Six Months to Get a Life

Ben Adams

Clink Street

London | New York

Published by Clink Street Publishing 2014

Copyright © Ben Adams 2014

First edition.

ISBN: 978-1-909477-49-0
Ebook: 978-1-909477-50-6

Wednesday 26th March

My decree absolute came through today. I am officially divorced.

I have never been divorced before. I thought it would feel different – either like being released from the proverbial life sentence, or maybe in my more pessimistic moments like being a discarded cigarette, cast adrift with the life sucked out of me. I didn't know whether to celebrate or cry. In the end I just changed my Facebook status to single and went off to work.

Despite my divorce, the world seems to be proceeding as usual. It is raining, the Russians and Ukrainians are arguing, the Northern line was packed and my fellow commuters were determined to get to work before me. Most managed it too. No one congratulated me on my divorce. No one seemed to notice that I wasn't wearing a wedding ring. Oh well, life goes on I suppose.

But what will life look like for a 42-year-old newly-divorced man with two kids? Am I destined to grow old alone, bitter and twisted with only the telly and the occasional visit from family I don't really know to keep me going? Or can I make a new life for myself that involves being a proper dad, going out, meeting new people and even getting the occasional bit of sex from time to time?

Tempting as it is to wallow in self-pity, spending the months to come immersing myself in soap operas and made-up dramas rather than acting them out myself, I have, this very day, decided that I will not feel sorry for myself. I will not be 'done to'. I won't mope around.

In exactly six months' time, on 26th September, I will be 43 years old. Birthdays aren't normally a big thing for me but this one will be. I am going to throw a party and invite everyone I know. Well, maybe everyone except my ex. And my friends are going to celebrate my new life with me. I am going to get a life in the next six months.

There, I have said it. If I say it enough times I might start believing it; which is why I am writing this diary. I am making myself a commitment, setting it down in black and white, that I will take control. I will get off my backside and make things happen. I will forge a new life for myself, one with my kids, with new friends and, who knows, maybe even a new love. I will sort my life out and I will do it by my birthday.

I am going to commit events to writing whenever I can, to make myself push on rather than letting life pass me by. And you, my mythical reader, can assist me. You can let me rant without interruption. If you like, you can be my therapist but I am not paying you. Feel free to kick me up the backside when you are reading this and you notice too much negativity. Don't go easy on me either. If you'll forgive me a football analogy, don't be Phil Neal to my Graham Taylor; 'do I not like that'. I don't want your loyalty. I want you to push me to get over my divorce and achieve a new life that is fulfilling and fun for me and my kids.

Just so that you get to know me a bit, and maybe even empathise with me, I will tell you a bit about me and my situation. My name is Graham Hope. I am a 42-year-old divorcee with two kids – Jack, fourteen, and Sean, twelve.

I did have a wife but I haven't got one now. I did have a great house in Raynes Park on the edge of leafy Surrey but I haven't got that now either.

I am no Brad Pitt or Harry Styles in the looks department, or any other department for that matter. I have a more 'lived in' look, with a big nose and teeth that belong to a 42-year-old man rather than a Barbie doll. I am no ugly fat mug either, mind.

I am currently living with my parents in Morden, at the end of the northern line and just past the end of civilisation. That's a double whammy if ever there was one. I am living with my parents. And I am living in Morden.

Am I bitter about my situation? Well, if truth be told, yes, sometimes I am. My divorce has forced a radical rethink of my dreams. Gone are the thoughts of growing old with my ex, travelling the world, seeing the sights and occasionally popping home to hear about Jack's latest move during the football transfer window and Sean's latest century for England. Now I have resorted to dreaming about my chances of pulling Kylie Minogue. OK, so the dreams still aren't too bad but the problems start when I wake up and realise my future isn't as mapped out as it used to be.

You will notice that I keep referring to 'my ex'. I have this thing about telling you her name. She is a person and until recently she was important in my life. I suppose as the mother of our children she is still important. But this diary is not about her; it is about me. If you want to read her diary then you are in the wrong place. If you want to sympathise with her then feel free but I won't be giving you any help. She does actually write a diary; at least she used to. I flicked through it once when I came across it when I was looking for her car keys in her handbag. The one comment that stuck in my mind was, 'Graham has a big ego and a small dick. I wish it was the other way around.'

Back to me; in the wake of my divorce I'm a little bit lonely, missing my kids when they aren't with me, worried about money and petrified about how long it will be before I feel loved again. In short, I have a long way to go to sort my life out. But on the positive side, I have some ideas. I might try internet dating as it could be a bit of a laugh, I am looking forward to saying 'yes' a few more times when my mates ask me out for a beer and ... actually I can't think of anything else positive at the moment.

My mates didn't ask me out for a beer tonight. There was no football on the telly either. So tonight I stayed in with my dad and drank London Pride out of a can, which is pretty much how I have spent most evenings since my wife and I went our separate ways (she didn't go anywhere but I came here). My dad has fallen asleep with his head on the table now, so I have been left in peace to give myself a pep talk.

Taking control of my life is a start, but if you take control of a car and don't know where you are going, you may well go round in circles or worse still end up in Morden. So I need to set some goals. The therapists on the telly are always telling people to have goals. So after much thought and another can of London Pride, here are mine. By my 43rd birthday I will:

1. Be a good dad
2. Get somewhere else to live
3. Get a social life
4. Get a more interesting job
5. Get some decent bottled lager in
6. Get fit

Now the more observant of you will have noticed that goals 5 and 6 might be somewhat conflicting. In my defence, I am not striving for perfection, only a normal life.

And I have six months to get it.

Thursday 27th March

My second day of being divorced was much like my first. In fact it was much like every day for the past year or so. My ex and I pretty much separated last Easter, albeit with the odd brief reconciliation in the winter months. We just drifted apart, like some couples do. There were no sordid affairs with naked people hiding in wardrobes when spouses come home unexpectedly. At least not that I know of. There were no frying pan-throwing tantrums or punch-ups. There were just two people not bringing the best out of each other. We didn't fight about who got the kids. We left it up to them and they decided to base themselves with their mum (I'm not bitter). We didn't even fight about who got the house. I consider myself to be more of a lover than a fighter, but as a newly single man, I am beginning to discover I don't do either very well.

Today I went to work like any other day. I wish I could tell you I have an exciting job – something like a brain surgeon, a football commentator or a travel reporter. But actually I work in an office shuffling papers. Work for me is a way of earning money to live my life. So today I earned some money that I will end up giving a chunk of to my ex. I'm not bitter.

'Short skirt Sarah' at work noticed I wasn't wearing my

wedding ring today. By my reckoning it has taken about four months for someone to notice, or pluck up the courage to comment. I actually took my ring off on Christmas day and chucked it at my ex in disgust at being bought a 'beard care set' for Christmas. I haven't even got a beard. 'It hurts when you kiss me,' she told me in her defence.

'I am surprised you can remember,' was my somewhat caustic response.

I was a bit tongue-tied around Sarah. It isn't that I'm particularly interested in her (obviously I wouldn't say no if she asked). It is just that I am a bit tongue-tied around women generally at the moment, especially when they are attractive. My communication skills when I am around women seem to be similar to those of a four-year-old with a speech impediment.

I definitely need to hone my response when someone comments on the lack of my wedding ring, as today's conversation didn't go swimmingly.

'Oh Graham, what's happened to your wedding ring?'

'Sarah, I took it off because I have been officially divorced for two days now, I am single and living with my parents and seeing my kids at weekends.'

Short skirt Sarah finished making her cup of tea rather quickly and left me alone in the kitchen. I guess my response was a bit overpowering, in the same way as an innocent 'How are you?' enquiry at the tea point might not be anticipating an 'I have cancer and only 4 weeks to live' response…

I remember when I used to be in with the drinking crowd at work. Every Friday night, most Friday lunchtimes and other nights too, I would get invited to various drinks to celebrate Fred's leaving, Emily's engagement, John's promotion, Gemma's new hairdo or Eamon's 'coming out party'. I am now considered too old to receive such invites, or maybe too married. We will see if they start flooding in to my inbox again now that I'm divorced.

On my way home from work I took a significant step forward in achieving one of my six goals. I bought six bottles of Stella. That's one goal ticked off and we are only one day in to my quest. Let's hope the other goals are just as easy to achieve.

I phoned home tonight to check in with the kids. Jack was out playing football and all I got out of Sean were a few grunts and a fairly unenthusiastic 'see you at the weekend'. What do I expect? They are teenagers, I suppose.

Just so you know, Jack is the obsessively competitive sporty child who will give any sport a go but particularly likes football and cricket. He's at that age where he is beginning to discover girls and as a consequence is conscious of his self-image (whereas I am at that age where I am forced to rediscover girls and am conscious of my self-image). Jack likes to 'fit in' and is embarrassed by anything that differentiates him from the norm, like having two parents who don't live together.

Sean, on the other hand, is less sporty. He does like cricket but he hasn't inherited the same competitive gene as his brother. He is more easy-going and less interested in what others think of him. He isn't afraid to make a few waves, either with what he says or what he does. He once joined a school knitting club because he wanted to make himself a hat. He is friends with anyone who has a Sony gaming device. Sean seems to be taking our family changes in his stride, on the outside at least. Both Jack and Sean are good kids, so far without too much attitude. But give it time…

Friday 28th March

Work was quiet today. Most people in my office 'work from home' on Fridays. I bought cakes for the few that were in and sent an email to everyone in the company telling them that there were cakes in the kitchen. That'll teach the bastards for starting their weekends early.

I made some small progress with goal six today. I went swimming after work. I hate swimming. I hate the whole experience of driving to the pool, getting changed in a cubicle you couldn't swing a wet pair of speedos in, messing about with a locker, swimming up and down without actually going anywhere and avoiding the annoying bloke who swims backstroke and expects you to dodge his flailing arms.

Why did I go swimming if I hate it so much? Well, I was getting ready for work this morning and noticed that my trousers were a bit tighter than they used to be. I found another pair in my wardrobe and tried them on but they were tight too. I must be putting on a few pounds. I suppose eating mum's butter-rich food and drinking dad's beer could have that effect on a man. Maybe I have always been a few pounds above my peak fighting weight but I haven't paid too much attention to the fact until now. I haven't been particularly self-obsessed until now. If I am to meet someone new, I don't want them to wince when I rip my shirt off. I am not trying to be a Stallone or a Schwarzenegger, but I wouldn't mind losing a few pounds and building up some muscle.

Morden swimming baths is, metaphorically speaking at least, a million miles from the posh private membership health clubs of Wimbledon. The paint is flaking off the tiles, the showers are rubbish and the toilets stink, but I can't afford luxury gym memberships these days.

I am not a bad swimmer, but within seconds of getting into the pool this evening I was reminded that I am not a particularly good swimmer either. Some ten-year-old squirt shot past me doing breast stroke while I was thrashing down the pool doing crawl. My trunks came down every time I pushed off from the end. I wouldn't have been too bothered about the trunks thing but for the fact that just after one of the most severe slippages, Sean's none-too-shabby form teacher complained to the lifeguard that it was putting her off her stroke. Sean, if you get a bad school report mate, I am sorry.

I am feeling slightly apprehensive at the moment. No, actually I am feeling scared stiff. My mates, who I was convinced had lost my number over the past few months, have eventually phoned and asked if I want to go out clubbing. Now this is probably where you start getting to know me. I like going to the pub as much as the next middle aged man does. In fact, I like nothing more than sitting in the Raynes Park Tavern or the Morden Brook having a few jars with friends. But what I have never liked, even when I was a young student, was going to night clubs. Are they even still called night clubs? Anyway, when it comes to dancing, I have something in common with horses – I have two left feet. Modern music makes me feel like I am about to have a heart attack, it is too loud and the bloody lighting in those places is normally so dim that I worry I might not find the toilets when I am desperate after a few pints.

So, back to tonight. I am going out with Dave, Ray and Andy. Dave is my cool mate. He is in a band so he knows his music. He loves his dancing and knows all the 'moves', whatever they are. He is a bit of a bragger and likes to tell people that he's a big-shot city dealer, but a few months ago I went into the bank on Threadneedle Street when I was up in the City and Dave was serving on the cashier desk. He used to be married but his wife left him for a librarian. He once told me he could have coped if she had left him for a famous pop star but he was a bit choked up for a year or two about the librarian thing. Dave is the stud of the group.

Ray is, according to my ex, hot. He is the sort of guy who always seems to be the centre of attention without having to try. Despite this, he has never really settled down but that doesn't seem to bother him.

And Andy is, like me, more reserved and considered in his actions. Some might even say he's boring but at least he will keep me company propping up the bar while the others are strutting their stuff on the dance floor tonight. Andy's wife died in a car accident a few years ago and he has never found anyone who can replace her. He is a genuinely nice guy who some woman would enjoy introducing to her mother over afternoon tea.

So tonight is four single blokes going out on the town. I do have happily married friends, but tonight is for single guys 'looking for action' as Dave puts it.

When I was at university, I used to go out of an evening with the aim of 'pulling a bird'. I rarely (actually never but don't tell my mates) succeeded. I haven't needed to 'pull' for the last fifteen-plus years but I am sure that, come this evening, I will slip seamlessly back into the old routine of making a fool of myself on the dance floor and coming home alone. The only difference between now and fifteen years ago is that this time I am more than likely to fall asleep on a train on the way home and end up in Effingham Junction or some other godforsaken place.

If I am going to meet a new woman over the next six months, it won't be on the dance floor. But I am going to go out anyway as Dave tells me I have got to put myself in the shop window.

Saturday 29th March

So, do you really want to know what happened last night? Can I just tell you I made a fool of myself and leave it at that? No, I thought not. OK, we went for a few beers in the Raynes Park Tavern. I was fine with this bit of the evening. I held my own in the banter stakes and even managed to have a few quick conversations with women ('four pints of lager please.' 'OK, coming right up'). Things went downhill rapidly though when we moved on to Wimbledon for part two of our evening's entertainment.

I hadn't been to a night club in years so I hadn't even given a thought to dress codes. I had a row with the bouncer who told me I couldn't come in wearing trainers.

'They aren't any old trainers, they're fucking expensive trainers,' I protested. Actually I would have been quite happy if the bouncer had sent me home but Dave slipped him a tenner and he let me in.

The club was as bad as I had feared it would be. The music was thump, thump, thump; the average age of the clientele was about fifteen (even with us there) and the strobe lighting did my head in. I know this is making me sound old but it is just the truth. Night clubs and I just do not mix.

I did my best to stay at the bar with Andy but even Andy ended up dancing. The traitor seriously let me down. Eventually Dave physically manhandled me on to the dance floor. Dave, Ray and Andy had managed to infiltrate a group of mature women out for a good night. I use the word infiltrate deliberately. To me the dance floor felt a bit like a war zone, with people parading their weapons, ready to engage the enemy at the slightest opportunity and eventually move in for the kill. I just worried I would be caught in the crossfire.

I did my best to wobble from foot to foot in time to the beat and once I had mastered that bit I even threw in the odd hip jerk or two.

Drinks came and went. Women came and went. Until eventually I looked around and realised to my horror that my mates were nowhere to be seen. They had deserted me. They should be shot. The woman dancing closest to me was looking at me with intense but slightly unfocussed eyes. To my untrained eye, her dancing was no better than mine. This bolstered my confidence further, to the extent that my dance moves became a bit more exaggerated. Suddenly I thought I was Tom Jones or Michael Jackson.

I was concentrating so much on my 'moves' and on the woman opposite me, who by this point looked like she was about to topple over, that I didn't notice the ring of people encircling us. I was just about to move in for some hand to hand combat with the lovely drunk woman when Dave tapped me on the shoulder.

'Mate, what the hell are you doing?' he asked.

'Piss off mate, I am in here,' I replied, somewhat irritated at being thrown of my stride.

'You're fucking twerking. Men don't twerk, especially fat blokes.'

It was at that point that I noticed the ring of on-lookers laughing hysterically and pointing at me. It was also at that point that my dance partner threw up all over my shoes. I got my coat and exited the battlefield with my white flag raised.

Where did last night get me? It reminded me how easy being married is. It got me poorer, it got me embarrassed and it got me a hangover. And it got me in trouble with my parents because for some reason I left my sick-encrusted shoes on the kitchen table.

I am missing my kids more than I am missing my wife. I mean my ex-wife. But I must confess that I wasn't particularly missing the kids first thing this morning when the doorbell rang and Jack and Sean turned up on my parents' doorstep. My first official single dad act was to try not to run to the loo and throw up within the first two minutes of the kids being there.

Only having my kids for the odd evening and weekends will take some getting used to. The general rule is that I get the kids every other weekend but we have agreed that, over and above the formal requirement, they can come and stay with me whenever they want. If this morning was anything to go by, that won't be very often. Still, things picked up as the morning went on. They played on the PS4. Maybe not the quality time the child psychologists might have in mind, but there isn't a PS4 at my ex's so that's one reason they'll want to come to my parents'.

The other reason they will want to come is to see the dog. Yes, my wife gets the house, the kids and the best car. I get the mortgage and the German shepherd puppy. Albus is his name, after Albus Dumbledore. If you don't know who he is, then where have you been for the past ten years?

I made some progress on goal one today – getting a new place to live. My parents threatened to throw me out if I didn't get off my arse and start sorting my life out. Well, it may not be the proactive progress I might have wanted, but I am one step closer to getting a place of my own – even if it might be a park bench.

Sunday 30ᵗʰ March

Living with my parents isn't easy. Having your old bedroom back more than twenty years after you left home and sharing the house with your parents is a big change from having your own kids, house, garden, telly and wife (yes, in that order). This significant step backwards in my life has taken some getting used to. I have to remind myself to abide by my parents' rules while in their house. Rules like washing up straight after a meal rather than when there aren't any clean dishes left in the cupboard, and cutting my toenails in the bathroom, not in front of the telly. Talking of the telly, I also have to make sure that the next time I watch Playboy TV when everyone else has gone to bed, I turn the channel back to BBC before I turn the TV off. Mum is still getting over the embarrassment of having her Women's Institute friends thinking she watches porn.

Having me as a lodger isn't easy for my parents either, especially at their age. They are both approaching their seventies. They are physically fit but my dad had a hip replacement last year and needs the other one doing too so he is temporarily less mobile than he would want to be. Mum could probably still climb a mountain faster than me and both of them can drink faster than me.

Before I moved in, they were very set in their ways. They

had a routine for what rooms in the house they would sit in at different times of the day (kitchen in the morning, conservatory in the afternoon, front room in the evening). Meals were served at one o'clock and six o'clock and after dinner they would listen to The Archers then move from the radio to the telly in time to watch the soaps. They would go to bed straight after the ten o'clock news.

Except for a short but explosive teenage stroppy period, I have always got on with my parents. We don't do cuddles and all that stuff, but pre-divorce, I used to go round there once a week with the family, have dinner, play board games and generally drink too much London Pride. I made another of my vows when I moved in with them. I wouldn't just use their house as a hotel. I would make the effort to continue spending quality time with them. This isn't proving easy.

'Quality time' these days seems to mean sitting around a kitchen table littered with empty London Pride cans and prosecco bottles, picking my life apart. Now anyone over the age of two would probably be capable of picking my life apart. But my mum and dad consider themselves uniquely qualified to do the job with a forensic precision. They were both social workers in their former lives. My mum used to do something worthy with the parents of children with dis-abilities and my dad used to manage a 'family services unit', whatever that means.

There is only so much frowning over my previous life choices or suggestions about future life choices that a man can take. I reached my limit today. Mum cooked a tradi-tional Sunday roast, beef and all the trimmings. We washed it down with our usual beverages. Our plates were empty, our stomachs full and our tongues alcoholically lubricated when mum asked me where it all went wrong.

'What do you mean 'where did it all go wrong'?' I asked.

'With your life, Graham. How did it come to this?' She

even did that palms up, arms outstretched hand gesture thing when she said 'my life', presumably meaning everything. Where did everything go wrong? Thanks mum, build me up, bolster my confidence.

I thought about going for a glib response but the earnest look on mum's face made me change track.

'I don't know mum, I guess my marriage just wasn't meant to last.' OK, so it wasn't exactly an insightful answer but it was the best I could do.

'That's nonsense and you know it, Graham,' mum continued. 'Marriages need to be worked at. It wasn't as if either of you had an affair or anything that drastic. Surely you could have worked through your differences?'

'You didn't even see a marriage guidance counsellor,' dad chimed in. We did actually but I hadn't told them about it because they would have had a go at me for walking out in the middle of a session.

And so it went on, two against one, tag-team wrestling. My parents still seem to think the sun shines out of my ex's backside. They act as if she is their daughter rather than me their son. They still hold out a hope that my perfect ex will have me back. I wouldn't go back even if she would have me back. Which she wouldn't.

I have told my parents time and again that my ex and I split up because of our terminal irritability with each other, our mutual intolerance of each other, our irreconcilable TV viewing schedules. We just didn't like each other. I tried to explain that to my parents but, to them, not liking your other half doesn't constitute grounds for divorce.

'You should have paid more attention to her when you had her,' dad advised. Why didn't I think of that?

'Those poor children,' mum offered. Why didn't I think of them too? I was on the ropes by this point, being seriously double-teamed by my parents, but wasn't about to submit.

'Bloody hell, will the two of you just leave me alone? I have had it with your sniping at me. You might have been married for ever but all you ever do is sit on your arses watching crap on the telly. I'd prefer to be single and living than married and dead.' The 'atomic drop', the 'full nelson' and the 'gorilla press' all combined into one move. That told them.

'Happy mother's day,' mum muttered as I was heading for the door. Shit.

At this point, I think I should make a confession. Being divorced, separated from my kids and my marital home (not to mention my ex) is quite stressful. It is quite a large upheaval in my life and may just have caused a slight emotional imbalance in my otherwise rock-solid equilibrium. In other words, I may be a bit self-centred at the moment, even a bit emotionally unstable. Not to the extent that I am about to charge around Morden with a lethal weapon killing random strangers, but enough that I may snap at my parents from time to time.

I need to put an end to alcohol-influenced conversations about my life.

Wednesday 2nd April

My mood was bolstered this afternoon when I found out that my ex had a stomach bug.

I miss my children. Just writing those words doesn't do the feeling justice. On the days that they aren't with me, i.e. most days, the first thing I think of when I wake up is what are they up to? Are they out of bed yet? What are they watching on the telly? What are they having for breakfast? Particularly at weekends I wonder whether they are out with their mates having fun, or sitting at home bored and wondering what their dad is up to.

I have been quite a good dad up until this point. As you will have gathered by now, I can be moody. I can even be angry and have absolutely on occasion been known to shout at my children. But generally, on balance, I don't think I have done a bad job as a dad.

I have always spent lots of time with the kids, going to watch countless football, rugby and cricket matches and taking them on loads of days out to the latest 'must-do' theme park. In our marital home I was in charge of holidays and we did the Florida Disney thing and had lots more fantastic holidays besides. I also genuinely enjoy Jack and Sean's company on rainy days in. I am telling you this so that you realise that, for me, undoubtedly the worst part of being divorced is being away from your children. So I was pleased my ex was ill because it gave me the opportunity to spend time with the kids when I got home from work. You didn't think I was just gratuitously pleased that she was suffering, did you?

Like most parents divorcing, I have had my fair share of heartbreaking conversations with the kids. The conversations with Jack and Sean were far more heart-wrenching than the conversations with my wife, which probably explains why we got divorced. We had another such conversation tonight.

I took my boys to Frankie and Bennys in Colliers Wood for tea. I needed the space away from my parents and thought the kids deserved a treat. We had a good time discussing everything from football to computer games to what fancy things we would buy if we won the lottery (Sean would have a waterslide going from his bedroom window to our own swimming pool and Jack would have a full-size football pitch with proper goals 'with nets and everything'). As the boys devoured their huge chocolate-laden puddings, Jack steered the conversation in an altogether more serious direction.

'Things are never going to be the same again, are they dad?'

'What do you mean, son?' I asked, even though I suspected I knew exactly what he meant.

'I hate us all not living together as a family anymore,' Jack explained. 'I hate the quiet in mum's house when you aren't there. I hate watching the telly without you. I even hate eating tea without you taking the mickey out of us trying to hide our vegetables under our knife and forks.'

'I hate going to bed without you mixing me up a story,' Sean joined in. I hadn't made up a bedtime story for him in years but I didn't bother pointing that out.

'I even hate it that you aren't there to call me smelly or Jackie,' my big boy said. 'Can't you come home?'

Both boys looked at me expectantly. They have asked me that question a few times before. I never know quite how to answer it. On one occasion I remember saying something along the lines of, 'Your mum and I don't love each other anymore so we can't live together.' That seemed like a perfectly reasonable answer to me but I don't think the kids could really get their heads around it.

The next time the question came up I tried emphasising the benefits of having two happier parents even if they lived in different houses. That response seemed to tick some boxes for Sean but even the prospect of getting double the amount of birthday and Christmas presents didn't sway Jack.

Tonight I went for the blunt approach because I had run out of alternatives.

'Your mum doesn't particularly like me anymore, boys, so I can't move back in.'

'She told us you don't like her,' Jack said.

'Maybe we don't like each other very much,' I conceded wearily.

And that, in a nutshell, is why we split up. Both answers are true. My ex doesn't really like me. I don't really like my ex. And when it comes to talking to the kids about it, we both find it easier to heap the blame on the other party.

Without wishing to get all defensive, I feel the need to justify my answer and I suppose by implication my ex's answer too. I can't tell the kids I don't like their mum because I don't want to give them permission not to like their mum. I suspect my ex's rationale is the same. She is generally a really good, conscientious parent who wouldn't want to give the kids tacit permission not to like me.

Life is hard. Divorced parents have to walk a real tightrope when trying to do the best for their children. I can only imagine how hard it must be when you throw anger into the mix. Luckily, there wasn't much anger when my ex and I split. It sounds hard to believe after fifteen years of marriage but we were too worn down to fight. We didn't care about each other enough to get angry.

I paid the bill and took the kids back to my parents', tucked them in to bed and mixed them up a story about a boy who won the lottery and built lots of fancy things in his garden.

Thursday 3rd April

Whenever Jack and Sean stay with me, my parents' house bursts at the seams. They live in a decent-sized terraced house with three bedrooms, but even before I moved in, the house was cluttered with the detritus that people accumulate over the course of their lives. There aren't enough drawers for the kids' clothes, they haven't got a wardrobe to use and as a consequence stuff gets strewn everywhere. Worse than that for the boys, they have to share a bedroom. Lots of children share bedrooms but my kids aren't used to it and them sharing normally ends in trouble.

As for the bathroom situation, the house only has one bathroom. We are all on a tight schedule during our morning routines. Why, then, does my dad, who is retired and does nothing but sit about all day, insist on having a shower at precisely the time that the boys and I need to use the bathroom? This morning I ended up being late for work and had to shout at the kids to hurry up.

When I got home my mum warned me that Jack was still in a mood.

'What's up with you?' I asked him when I eventually found him throwing a tennis ball at the wall behind my dad's shed.

'I got two detentions at school today,' he informed me.

'Two. I have never got a detention in my life and today I get two.'

When I asked him what he did to deserve the detentions, he went off on one.

'What I did to deserve a detention was be born to parents who couldn't keep their marriage together. Instead of living in a happy family, sometimes I live somewhere where I can't get into the bathroom until nearly lunchtime which makes me late for registration. That's detention number one. And then when I eventually get to school I realise that because I live in two houses I have forgotten which house my geography book is in. It's at my mum's but because I am already late for school I don't have time to go to mum's to get it. So I get given my second detention for not doing my geography homework because my stupid geography teacher doesn't believe that I have actually done it but left it at mum's.'

And breathe. I could have told Jack that he should have got up earlier to get in to the bathroom and checked his school bag the night before school to make sure he had all his books but sometimes you need to give a kid a break. I accepted full responsibility for Jack's predicament and apologised to him. I want to be there for him when he needs a shoulder to cry on.

I know I shouldn't have on a school night but I took the kids off to watch Gravity at the cinema (it might have won Oscars but we got bored with watching Sandra Bullock floating around in space).

Friday 4th April

When the kids were born, my parents fully embraced their role as grandparents. They used to spoil Jack and Sean rotten, buying them presents, feeding them sweets, letting them stay up late on sleepovers at their house and generally leaving any disciplining that needed to be done to us.

At some point over the last few months the dynamic has shifted a bit, to the extent that Jack and Sean sometimes could be forgiven for thinking that they have got four parents.

'What's for tea?' Jack asked within five minutes of getting back from playing football in the park with his mates.

'Kippers,' my mum replied, 'and I hope you are going to shower first.'

'Kippers, yuk! They stink. Can't we have something else?' he protested.

'You can eat what you are given,' dad snapped.

And things didn't get better as the evening progressed. The boys were variously told off for playing football in the garden and breaking most of mum's daffodils, walking mud into the lounge, not flushing the toilet and leaving lights on. At least they didn't cut their toenails in front of the telly. My parents are running out of patience after being around the kids for the last few days. As far as I am concerned, the boys' misdemeanours this evening were all fairly low level, but it isn't my house so I couldn't really intervene with my parents on their behalf. Eventually Jack snapped at my dad.

'I hate you. I hate your stupid house and I hate your stupid kippers. I wish I didn't have to stay here.'

I was with Jack on the latter part of his outburst at least.

The boys and I had another of our man-to-man chats. I told them how hard it must be for my parents to go from living on their own to having us rabble invading their space and routines. I then told them of my intention to get somewhere to live where we could have our own space.

'I know we don't stay with you as much as we stay with mum but it isn't easy when you live here,' Jack said. 'We will stay with you more when you get your own place.'

Jack has always been worried that I would take the fact that he and his brother were spending more time with their mum than with me as an indication that they loved her more than they loved me. To be honest I struggled, or maybe that should be struggle, not to see it that way. I try my best not to show it to the kids, though.

'You will take the PS4 with you when you go, won't you?' Sean added. Nice to know where I stand in the order of priorities.

Saturday 5th April

My ex was well enough to take the kids back today. She phoned up and asked me to send them home. I could have argued with her; weekends are my time with the boys. But I thought the boys would probably want to go home after Jack's outburst at my mum yesterday, so I sent them on their way. Things will be different when I get my own place.

My sister Hilary turned up after the kids had gone. My sister and I have led slightly different lives over the years. Whereas I have been your model of conventional behaviour, Hills has ploughed a different furrow. She had her first baby at seventeen and her second at nineteen. The father, or was it fathers, remained anonymous. She did get married for a while when in her twenties but that union didn't last long. Hilary had a couple more kids before eventually deciding that she preferred the company of women. She has been living with her current partner, Donna Anchor, for quite a while now. They have an old 'Hope and Anchor' pub sign hanging outside their front door.

Hills is about three years younger than me. I got on with her fine when we were kids. She went through a phase of wanting to be like me. No, that's wrong: she wanted to be better than me. When my mates weren't around we would play football and tennis in the street together. She would tackle harder and run faster, not being content until she had beaten me. Sometimes, despite being younger than me and dare I say it, being a girl, she would beat me too.

I didn't mind the competition with Hills when my mates weren't around but when my mates were there, Hills still wanted to play with us. That was often truly annoying.

As we got older and she stopped idolising her big brother, we drifted apart. She became more opinionated and stroppy and wouldn't let me push her around like I used to. Her interest in boys began to dominate her life and as far as I could tell she was the first in her group of friends to start wearing short skirts and revealing tops. I may well have found some of Hilary's outfits attractive on other teenagers at the time but having your sister wear them was a tad embarrassing, especially when my mates started commenting on her body.

I was at university when she got pregnant the first time. And the second time for that matter. Andy told me at the time that everyone speculated about the identity of the first baby's father. Dave's name was mentioned but he has always denied ever sleeping with my sister.

Hills and I have kept in touch over the years but we don't see each other that regularly. We still do this thing whenever we meet up where she tries her best to outdo me. It is a bit like a game of 'top trumps' with our lives. 'I've got a better car than you,' she would say. 'My kids are getting better grades at school than yours,' I would respond. My parents, who are ultra-traditional, have normally come down on my side in these games of top trumps but tonight my dear sister took great pride in blowing me out of the water.

'I've been in a stable relationship for ages now but look at you, you're over forty and you're living with mum and dad. Your life's a shambles.'

'It's not a shambles. I am just in a period of transition,' I tried.

'Period of transition? Listen to yourself; are you sure you aren't Adrian Mole and Bridget Jones's lovechild?' she asked. Rather cruelly, I thought.

Sunday 6th April

I got a call bright and early this morning from Jack. The boys wanted to come over for the day. That pleased me, not just because it felt like I had won a small victory over my ex but because I didn't have a clue what I would have done all day if the boys hadn't chosen to come to spend time with me. It is amazing how quickly I can recoup my 'dad energy'.

When I see the children, I always wrestle with the dilemma of whether to ask them how their mother is. On the one hand I think they might resent it if I didn't ask, as they naturally feel that their father should be concerned about how their mother is getting on. But on the other hand, I don't want to appear to be too interested in case it encourages them to think that there might still be some future for the four of us together as a family. There certainly isn't.

I asked Sean how mum was this morning, mainly because I was conscious that she was still recovering from her stomach bug. Judging by his reply, it would seem that my ex's stomach bug is well and truly history.

'She's good dad. She went out with some guy last night and she was singing along with the radio this morning so she obviously had a good night.'

'What time did she get back last night?' I asked.

'Don't ask me, I was asleep.'

Here we go then. It is easy to say things like my marriage to my ex reached its natural end and that I am over her. It is easy to say it; but is it the truth? Before today I honestly didn't think I would be jealous if my ex started a new relationship but after my conversation with Sean, I know I was wrong. I am jealous. Why did my ex bother asking for the boys to go back to her yesterday if she was only going to go out last night? Who looked after the boys?

It took all my effort to stop myself from giving Sean the third degree about this bloke. 'What did he look like?' 'How tall was he?' 'What sort of car did he drive?' 'Was he a snappy dresser?' 'Was he a dick?' Somehow I managed to keep my inquisitiveness to myself.

I know I am massively jumping ahead of events here, but I am now struggling to keep images of my wife in bed with a new man out of my head. She may not sleep with this particular bloke but she is bound to find someone to share her bed with at some point.

Why am I feeling jealous? Or more particularly, who am I jealous of? The more I think about it, I am not jealous of the bloke who went out to dinner with and will potentially sleep with my ex. I think I am jealous of my ex because she has found herself someone to go out with. She has found herself a prospective new partner before I have.

When the kids were upstairs, I got my phone out and found my ex on Facebook. Since we separated I had wondered about deleting her as a friend but I am not sure what the protocol is here. If I delete her does that smack of the act of a bitter and twisted man? Or should I keep her as a friend because she is the mother of my children? Anyway, this morning I was glad I hadn't deleted her.

I looked through her activity. She doesn't update her profile very often and hadn't posted anything about going out to dinner with a new bloke. Her last profile update just said 'off to have my hair cut'. I looked to see if she had any new friends but couldn't find any tall, dark, handsome new bloke there either.

I could hear the kids shouting at me for something or other so I hurriedly put the phone away. I should probably defriend my ex, otherwise I worry I will keep peeking at her activity for years to come. Sometimes I wish I could work my real-life relationships in a Facebook-enabled way: just press a few keys and my emotions relating to any given person would immediately switch off.

Once I'd got over the news of my ex's dinner date, Sean and I went to watch Jack's Sunday league football cup final. Well, I say Sean went to watch his brother but he spent most of his time going to the café down the road with his best mate Robert, who had just finished his game. We took the puppy with us.

Albus is a great dog. My ex and I got him in October during one of our brief reconciliations. With the benefit of hindsight this was one of our more ridiculous decisions. My ex's rationale for getting him was that it would give the family a joint project. We could walk him together, share responsibility for training and grooming him. My rationale was more realistic. At least the dog would wag its tail and be genuinely pleased to see me when I get back from work.

Albus was a tiny pup when we took him home, only nine weeks old. He was an instant hit with the kids but didn't quite manage to achieve our unspoken and totally unrealistic hope of saving our already doomed marriage. By the time he was six months old, my wife had become my ex.

In the six months that we have had him, he has gone from being a tiny pup to a huge beast of a pup. He still has some growing to do, despite already being able to put his paws on the kids' shoulders and lick their faces. I have given up reminding the boys that they don't know where the dog's tongue has been. Actually it isn't true anyway; we know perfectly well where his tongue has been.

Jack's team were playing the league champions. In pursuance of my admittedly stop-start (more stop than start) attempt to get fit, I decided to jog around the pitch with the dog while I was watching the game. I managed about two laps before I got a stitch and had to stop to recover.

Somehow, when I was bent double trying to regain my breath, I let go of the lead and Albus invaded the pitch. He went straight for the ball, grabbed it in his teeth and ran in and out of players evading capture. I tried calling him but he just wouldn't come. We have still got work to do with him on the training pitch.

It was like the scenes you see on a telly when the stewards are trying to capture a streaker. Eventually Sean got him back by offering him a bit of the sausage out of his hot dog.

Sean was in hysterics. Jack was mortified.

'Dad, what did you let him off for?' he shouted at me from across the pitch.

I acted all apologetic but actually I quite admire the dog. He just sees something he wants and goes straight for it. He's got no inhibitions. I wish I was a bit more like him sometimes. Maybe if I was, I would be able to find myself a new woman and have the balls to approach her.

Jack lost his football so he was in a foul mood for the rest of the day.

Tuesday 8th April

Albus is in the spotlight at the moment. Today my beloved father turned his scorn onto him. It wasn't as if Albus was chewing up their best cushions or anything. The best cushions are in the front room and the cushions he was chewing up were in the kitchen.

I have spent this evening doing mundane chores. Despite being 'on my own' for a while now, I am still struggling with doing some things for myself. In my former marital home my ex would do most of the domestic chores. This wasn't because I am a chauvinist pig, but simply because I worked longer hours than her. It's not as if I didn't lift a finger around the house (I feel like I am being a tad defensive again here). I know my way around the kitchen and can make a mean curry. I can even use the washing machine and know how to operate a washing line. But ironing is a different matter altogether. In my marital home I tested out and proved correct the Jack Duckworth theory that if you cock it up enough times, someone will do it for you. It was almost worth staying married to my ex because she did the ironing, but the marriage guidance counsellor told me that wasn't reason enough to stay with her, so I didn't. What did she know anyway?

Since my divorce, I have repeatedly tried to cock up the

ironing but my parents are proving that every good theory has an exception. With the days heating up, I am not sure how much longer I can cope with wearing jumpers to cover up my latest inept attempt to iron a shirt. And the manufacturers that claim their shirts are non-iron or easy-iron should be sued for talking bollocks or whatever the technical term is.

When I wasn't doing the ironing I was working my way through my old music collection - a collection I have hardly listened to or expanded since the 80s. Growing up in that halcyon decade, I was too young for punk and too old for rap. Anything 'alternative' left me cold. So pop and soft rock it is. The kids take the piss out of me constantly. Occasionally, in a token effort to look even vaguely cool, I will try something new. I thought I was being progressive when I bought an Adele album but that didn't get me any street cred, nor did Bruno Mars. I did get some grudging respect when I took Jack and Sean to the Capital FM Summertime Ball last year, until when we got there I didn't recognise any of the acts. So I gave up trying to keep up with the kids and now just listen to my extensive back catalogue. Today I immersed myself in my youth and listened to 'The Joshua Tree' by U2 over and over again.

Wednesday 9th April

Divorce doesn't half play havoc with your finances. As a couple my ex and I were doing pretty OK, at least in financial terms. My job might be mind-numbingly boring but it does at least come with a half-decent salary. My ex worked too. We had only recently moved into our detached house in Surrey. OK, the house wasn't a million miles from the local council dump and is only in Surrey rather than London by a matter of metres, but when all's said and done it's still a detached house in Surrey.

We used to go on decent holidays and generally didn't have to count the days before our salaries were paid in to our bank accounts. But now, following the dreaded 'D' word, I am not sure how I get myself into a position where I can afford to even rent a home on the commercial market suitable for a dad with an occasional two kids, let alone get myself back on to the property ladder.

My dad didn't help matters today when he suggested that it's about time I started paying rent. I am trying to save my pennies, the pennies that I am not giving to my ex, in the hope that sometime soon I will be able to afford to rent somewhere. If I have to pay my dad rent then it will take me longer to move out. I explained this logic to him but he was nonplussed.

A part of me suspects that my parents are trying to push me in to moving back with my ex. I keep telling them it won't happen but they aren't easily put off.

Thursday 10th April

I don't normally feel like a gooseberry around my parents but I did tonight. It's their wedding anniversary and they spent the whole evening banging on about the day they first met, their relationship and why their marriage has lasted so long.

'How long were you married for?' mum asked me at one point.

'What does it matter?' I responded. 'It's over now.'

I get the impression that my parents see my divorce as a black mark against me, an indication that I am not a great person. Maybe I'm not. I made my excuses and left them to it as soon as I had swallowed my last mouthful of beef Wellington.

My marriage might not have worked out but I don't regret getting married. My union with my ex produced the two best things in my life, my boys.

Mum and dad's wedding anniversary made me think a fair bit about my ex. As I have said before, this diary isn't about her but she was part of my life for fifteen years so I can't ignore her altogether.

Somewhat unconventionally we met outside a sexually transmitted diseases clinic in Roehampton. I got lucky one night. Not being a seasoned professional, I took my eye off the ball. Or balls. They subsequently itched so badly that I waddled off to the STD clinic. As I began the drive home I was rather distracted (they had seen fit to give me a 'routine' AIDS test too) and crashed smack bang into the woman who was later to become my ex. Literally smack bang.

'What the fuck do you think you're doing? Are you blind?' she shouted at me.

'Sorry, I was scratching my balls.'

As well as exchanging pleasantries, we exchanged phone numbers for insurance purposes. After a few beers a couple of nights later I phoned her up, and although it may stretch the imagination a bit, we ended up getting together.

In the first few weeks of our burgeoning relationship we met up most evenings after work, walked along the river, drank in different pubs and ate out at every opportunity. We were love's young dream.

On account of my sexually transmitted infliction it took a while before the relationship progressed to 'staying in'. My lovely ex insisted on seeing a clean bill of health signed in triplicate by a surgery full of doctors before she would go anywhere near my nether regions. And I never did find out what she was doing at the clinic.

We were married within a few months. Morden registry office pulled out all the stops. My dad snored loudly throughout my father-in-law's wedding speech, but no one blamed him because it was a mind-numbingly boring speech. We had a great day.

Fifteen years of marital bliss followed. I wish. In reality it was more like a few weeks of bliss and fourteen-plus years of more lows than highs. Our honeymoon was a high point, as were our children's births, although I was already having doubts about our relationship by the time Sean was born.

The woman I had fallen in love with seemed to have disappeared fairly quickly after our wedding, to be replaced by an intense character who was either on top of the world or completely stressed and miserable. The times when she was on top of the world were great but unfortunately they weren't very frequent and didn't last long when they did occur.

The rows we had were quite intense in the early days too, complete with raised voices and the odd projectile hurled in my general direction. She once picked up an apple from the fruit counter in the green grocers and threw it at me. It missed me and hit some poor unsuspecting old woman on the back of the head. Poor Granny Smith. I can't even remember what I had or hadn't done that made her throw the apple in the first place.

As our relationship wore on, the rows diminished, not because we were getting on better but because we didn't have the energy or the passion to argue. My ex gradually became more and more withdrawn until eventually, a couple of years ago, the doctors diagnosed depression and prescribed her some pills. The pills did help my ex to regain her equilibrium. The lows were less low. Her relationship with the kids improved but the damage to our relationship had already been done. We couldn't rekindle the passion we once had for each other.

For the record, our marriage lasted for fifteen years and two months.

Friday 11ᵗʰ April

Today, my mum made liver and bacon for tea. I am sure it is a generational thing, but I haven't had liver since, er, I last lived with my parents twentyplus years ago.

I am getting the feeling that, just like my marriage, living with my parents isn't going to end well. It didn't end well when I was a teenager either. I went to university and once I had completed my degree (talking bollocks for three years, more commonly known as politics) I moved back home. I stayed for about three days before I had an argument with my dad and moved out. My dad wanted me to eat some left-over cheese for tea whereas I wanted a take-away curry. We had a row and I moved in with my then girlfriend. Looking back on it, my girlfriend at the time was living in nurses' accommodation so I don't know why I hadn't thought of moving in with her sooner.

The decision to ban my parents from having conversations with me about my life has had an unintended consequence. I am beginning to get fitter. With nothing to talk about, and no desire to sit and watch episodes of Pointless, Countdown or Coronation Street on Sky Plus or to listen to The Archers on the radio, I have ended up drinking less beer and actually dusting off my dad's exercise bike. There is still a long way to go before I enter the Tour de France or even before I would confidently be able to cycle to the corner shop without getting a sweat on. The beer belly doesn't seem to be diminishing yet, but at least the journey has started.

It was a Friday night and yet I retreated to the sanctuary of my bedroom, put my headphones on and immersed myself in some classic Bon Jovi. 'You Give Love a Bad Name' really cheered me up.

Saturday 12th April

As Jack's football season has finished, the kids and I decided to do something a bit different today. We went swimming in London's Olympic pool. We fully immersed ourselves in the Olympics when they were here and were lucky enough to get tickets to see both Mo Farrah's gold medal-winning runs.

Fifty metres is a long way to swim without being able to touch the side, especially when your trunks keep falling down (I had forgotten about that issue until I got into the water). The kids and I had a few races. We would have re-enacted moments of British 2012 golden glory in the pool but there weren't any in the Olympics and we couldn't remember the names of any of our Paralympic winners so we just raced each other instead. Sean won, much to his brother's annoyance.

For lunch we decided to gorge ourselves on pizza. I appreciated the pizza more than the conversation. The kids spent the whole time haranguing me about my dress sense.

'Just look at what you're wearing, dad,' Jack started off. 'Your jeans are baggy and need chucking out.'

'And even if they weren't baggy you are too fat to be wearing jeans,' Sean joined in.

'Why have you got your t-shirt tucked in? Dad, you've got no swag.' Jack.

'Swag?' I asked, not having a clue what they were on about.

'And those trainers dad, we aren't going running so why are you wearing them?' Jack again.

'Because they are comfortable,' I tried.

'I suppose they're better than his flip flops,' Sean threw into the mix. 'And those tracksuit bottoms you wear to the pub just look stupid, dad.'

'People of your age should never wear tracksuits.' Jack again.

Alright, enough already. I let the kids take me to Westfield on the way back from the Olympic park and help me pick out a new pair of chinos, some designer leather shoes and a smart jacket. In return for their 'help', I bought them a designer jacket each too. I probably spent as much in the shopping centre as I would have spent on my first month's rent for a flat.

It has to be said that this isn't the first time I have spoilt the kids since our divorce. When I was married, I would always be the voice of reason. Have you eaten your fruit? Have you brushed your teeth? Have you done your homework? Have you tidied your bedroom? Now, I buy the kids 'Superdry' jackets, take them to Frankie and Bennys and to the cinema on school nights, let them have drinks in the front room (albeit not my lounge) and let them stay up later than is probably good for them. I know I am spoiling them but they have had a rough time lately. Doesn't everyone deserve a bit of spoiling from time to time?

Sunday 13ᵗʰ April

I dropped the kids back to my ex's at lunchtime today because I was going out for the afternoon. She wasn't best pleased when she saw their new jackets.

'Why have you bought them new coats? They have got plenty of coats already.'

'These aren't just any old coat. They're 'Superdry' jackets,' I told her as if I was suddenly the world's expert on designer clothing. 'And nice haircut, by the way.'

'I don't give a shit if they're Superman's jackets. The boys didn't need a new jacket.'

My ex is always practical. She is a 'needs' person not a 'wants' person.

'These must have cost a fortune,' she continued.

'They weren't cheap,' I conceded.

My ex ushered the boys inside before carrying on our conversation.

'Don't think I can't see what you're trying to do here, Graham. You are just trying to outdo me in the eyes of the children.'

'I just bought them a new jacket each. It's hardly the crime of the century,' I protested.

'If you've got money to burn on new things that the kids don't need then you can give me more maintenance because

I am struggling to pay for groceries, let alone designer cloth-ing,' my ex suggested.

I left it at that and made my exit. She may well have got the better of me in that one, although the maintenance point was a cheap shot. Two jackets cost nothing when compared to the new car my ex bought only weeks after we split up.

As well as dividing their possessions, divorcing couples also have to divide their friends. In mine and my ex's case, virtually all of our friends seem to have stuck by my ex but fallen by the wayside as far as my social calendar goes.

I made the mistake of discussing this unequal distribution of friends with Dave and Ray a while back. I came up with an explanation that centred around my ex forming most of the friendships over coffees at playgroups, nurseries and the school run and the men just being the 'plus ones' who went where they were told. In other words, my lack of friends was all down to me having to go to work whilst my ex was staying at home.

'No, Graham, all your mutual friends have taken your wife's side because you are a miserable dick.' Dave put me straight in his own inimitable way.

I think I will stick with my explanation. I got on fine with the blokes whose wives did school runs. We even went for the odd 'dads' night out', normally for a few beers and a curry. I just haven't got around to phoning them up to organise anything since my wife became my ex. With my ex and her mother's union mates organising us men's social calendars over the years, I am a bit out of practice.

Luckily, Katie and Bryan Green are the exception to the rule. They have kept in touch with me despite Katie know-ing my ex via anti-natal classes and Bryan and I being the 'plus ones'. The Greens invited me to a dinner party this afternoon at their trendy Southfields house.

As I walked along Replingham Road towards the Greens'

Georgian terraced abode, I couldn't help worrying that my ex might be on her way there too. I haven't seen her out socially since our split. This is hardly surprising as I haven't actually been out socially that often lately.

Katie and Bryan greeted me at the door. As they led me through their high-ceilinged hall, lined with portraits of people I didn't recognise hung in gold-leaf picture frames, I took a quick glance at the coats on the coat hooks. I couldn't see anything my ex owned. This was a good sign.

We went through in to their deep red painted dining room. The room was sparsely furnished, containing only a stone fire place, dark wood dining furniture and double doors that led out on to an immaculately laid out albeit quite compact garden. The table was laid for six. Other than Katie, Bryan and me, there were three people in the room, none of whom was my ex. I sighed inwardly. And maybe outwardly too.

I mentioned my relief to Bryan.

'Your ex has been to the last few dinners we have hosted but we thought we would have a change and invite you to this one,' Bryan informed me. Thanks mate.

Katie played the hostess with the mostess and introduced the three other people to me. I vaguely knew John and Tracey, him quiet and reserved, her more boisterous and opinionated. I had never met the third person before though; a woman whose name I didn't catch when Katie introduced us.

I will call her Miss Putney. I couldn't bring myself to ask her to repeat her name. The longer the conversation went on, the more awkward it became for me to ask her. So I didn't. I do remember where she lived though, hence the Putney reference.

Despite being anxious, bordering on a nervous wreck, for the whole evening, I don't think I embarrassed myself too much in front of Miss Putney. As the drink kicked in, Katie and Tracey talked enough for the six of us so the awkward silences between myself and Miss Putney were kept to a minimum.

I know this isn't exactly a ringing endorsement but she isn't an unattractive woman. She is tanned and has got a great smile but I couldn't help wondering why she had gone for a mullet hairstyle. She is nearly as tall as me and, like me, she could probably do with losing a few pounds. She wouldn't necessarily stand out in a crowd, but nor would I except that I would be the only bloke in the crowd dressed in chinos and trainers (I broke the lace on my posh shoes as I was putting them on and didn't have a spare one).

Anyway, the food was interesting too. We were served stuffed peppers for a starter followed by mushroom risotto. The trouble was that it tasted as though the risotto mixture had been used to stuff the peppers, the result being that the main course just tasted like the starter only without the peppers.

At the end of the evening the two couples and two singles present even started talking about whose turn it was to host the next gathering. I need a place of my own. Miss Putney and I swapped numbers. Even though I fear that we did it out of duty rather than any actual desire to talk to each other again, that has to be some kind of result, right?

Tuesday 15th April

It has been a while, if you know what I mean. My evening with married adult company on Sunday has reminded me what I am missing out on. It isn't just the sex, although I am certainly missing that. I haven't yet resorted to looking at dodgy websites on the iPad but that is only because the ex got the iPad and I don't think I would dare misuse my parents' tablet in that way. What Sunday night showed me is that, even more than the sex, I am missing the company, the sharing, the banter, the caring for each other. Some people might be able to convince themselves that they are happy being single. I don't think I am one of those people.

And there is no end in sight either. Miss Putney was nice but I am not excited about my prospects there. I am not a natural when it comes to charming the opposite sex. I am not bad at a bit of harmless flirting but am rubbish at 'sealing the deal' – does that sound too crude? Without going into any sordid detail, I did OK as a late teenager and into my twenties. My bedpost wouldn't be riddled with notches, but it is quality rather than quantity that counts, right? Actually some of the quality may have been a bit questionable too at times.

I am now well and truly middle aged. I don't meet new people. If I did meet new people I wouldn't know what to say to them. And the more attractive they are, the harder it is to talk to them. Why is that? If I was to meet a woman, it wouldn't be long before I uttered one or probably all of the following sayings – 'I am divorced'; 'I have two children but they live with their mum'; and 'Do you come here often?'

This evening was a case in point. I met someone when I was walking Albus on Wimbledon Common. 'Met' might be putting it a bit strongly but hey, if there is a straw to be clutched at, why not clutch it? Dog-walkers often talk to each other but it doesn't normally go beyond 'how old is he?' or if you are really lucky 'wow, she has got a beautiful coat'. Well, today I saw a woman who I have seen and exchanged nods with a few times before. Albus helped me out by urinating on her little pooch's head. If that isn't able to start a conversation between owners, I don't know what will.

'Your dog just weed on my dog's head,' dog-walking woman said to me with a smile. A lovely smile too.

'Oh, sorry. Do you come here often?' I am useless. It's official. I need to rehearse a few clever lines just in case I meet her again. She was 'top totty' as Dave would say.

Thursday 17ᵗʰ April

The cricket season has started. I just spent my first evening of the year at Sean's cricket training in Worcester Park. Despite not knowing anything about cricket, my ex other half used to do the cricket run because a couple of members of her mothers' union would also go with their children. Tonight, though, my ex asked me to take Sean because she had to work late.

I gladly agreed, partly because any opportunity to spend time with Sean is to be welcomed and partly because the cricket club has a cheap bar.

I sat out on the patio with Sarah and Debbie, both mums of Sean's friends and part of my social life pre-divorce. We had a good time gossiping about the kids and life in general. My normal nerves when speaking to women were nowhere to be seen, because I knew Sarah and Debbie's husbands and wasn't trying to hit on their wives. I could just be myself and didn't have to try to impress anyone.

'How are you doing, Graham?' Sarah asked me at one point when Debbie had gone off to the loo.

'Oh, I am doing really well. Life is good at the moment. I never seem to have a minute to myself. I don't know why we didn't divorce sooner.' I hate to think what I would have said had I been trying to impress Sarah.

'Have you thought what you would do if she ends up moving back to Exeter?' she asked from leftfield.

When I looked surprised, Sarah tried to backtrack but I wouldn't let her. It turns out that my ex's dad is ill and my ex has talked about pulling up sticks and moving to Exeter to be nearer him.

I told you that the ex and I didn't argue much. We might not have done when we were married, but we seem to be arguing more now we are divorced. When I dropped Sean back off at my old family home, I could barely wait for Sean to go inside the house before I confronted her on the doorstep.

'What's this I hear about you thinking about moving to Exeter?'

'What? Oh, I have thought about it,' My ex replied. 'Dad is ill and mum could do with some support.'

'Well feel free to go but if you think you are taking my kids with you, you've got another think coming.'

Diplomacy was never my strong point, particularly after a few beers. Unfortunately the direct approach rarely worked with my ex. In fact it probably pushed her closer towards moving than she previously was.

'If I decide to go to Exeter then I will take the kids with me,' she said. 'And there is nothing you could do to stop me.'

As if her words weren't clear enough, my ex's response was accompanied by a few vicious finger jabs to my chest to help emphasise her point.

'I don't want to go to Exeter,' Jack said from somewhere inside the house.

Responsible parents wouldn't have been rowing in front of their kids. I confess, though, that Jack's intervention on my side made the row almost worthwhile. Now that I have left them to it, I am sure that my ex will be smoothing things out with the kids. They would hate to move to Exeter though. There is nothing wrong with Exeter itself, but all the boys' friends are here. And I am here. I would like to think that this would count for something in their minds.

Thinking selfishly for a minute, I don't know what I would do if Jack and Sean moved to Exeter. It's hard enough to deal with them living down the road.

Saturday 20th April

Hot on the heels of Sean's first cricket practice came Jack's first cricket match.

Jack plays for a club that has links to his school. Most of the team are Jack's classmates. My boys don't play for the same club because Sean got fed up with everyone comparing his performances with those of his older brother.

We had an early hiccup when Jack was getting ready for the game and realised he had left his cricket box at his mum's. He refused point blank to wear his brother's.

'Dad, there is no way I am wearing that thing, I know where it's been,' he said emphatically.

'Just put it on and stop being an arse,' I told him.

'No way, it smells. And besides, Sean's got a chode. His box won't fit me.'

I had to look up the meaning of the word 'chode'. Apparently it means a short, fat penis that's wider than it is long. I am now thankful that no one has called me a chode yet in my life.

Because secondary school children are more independent and don't need to be taken to school, or maybe because my ex isn't around to organise me, I haven't got to know many of the parents of the other boys at Jack and Sean's school. I took pot luck and stood on the boundary next to a dad who

I vaguely recognised. We got chatting about the game and at one point when I clapped Jack for a diving stop on the boundary, the guy asked if I was Jack's dad. I nodded. He introduced himself as Geoff, the wicket keeper's dad.

Apparently Jack and Geoff's son Joe have been spending a lot of time together at school. Joe's parents got divorced last year and Joe splits his time between his mum and his dad. Jack got to hear about Joe's arrangement and has been asking Joe about it.

'My Joe is a good kid,' Geoff said. 'I am sure he has been helping your Jack through his situation.'

It is a bit disconcerting to have other people know your business but I am glad Jack has found someone to talk to about things if that's what he needs. We all need someone to talk to, I guess.

I asked Jack about it after his team had reached their victory target and the various groups of parents and players had gone their separate ways.

'Joe's OK,' he confirmed. 'His situation is a bit different from ours though.'

'How so?' I asked.

'His mum has moved in with another man. Joe hates him and wants to live with his dad.'

'What would you do if your mum decided to move in with that man she went out to dinner with a couple of weeks ago?' I asked Jack. I still can't quite get that thought out of my mind.

'Oh she won't, dad,' Jack told me. 'I heard her moaning to someone on the phone the other night that she had phoned him three times and he hadn't returned her calls.'

Shame.

Monday 21ˢᵗ April

It would seem that working all day, nearly having two kids, trying to get fit, having the occasional few beers with your mates, walking the dog and writing this diary are not enough to fill my days. Or so I am told by my dad, who thinks I need to get a hobby. True, despite it being a bank holiday I didn't do a lot today other than hang around the house listening to Bruce Springsteen but who is my dad to talk? All he does is trawl through the set top box catching up with daytime telly every evening. I sometimes wonder what he watches in the daytime.

As the afternoon turned to evening, Dave put me out of my misery and suggested we have a few down the Brook. I accepted willingly, thinking I might as well wallow in self-pity with Dave and a few pints as sit on my own in my room listening to depressing 80s music.

The 'Morden Brook' is our local boozer. It is an oasis in the desert that is the 1930s-built Morden suburbia. As an added bonus, the clientele won't normally punch you unless they have had one too many on a Saturday night.

As soon as our first pints were in front of us, I started on my litany of woes. I was working my way through my current living arrangements when Dave stopped me in my tracks.

'Mate, give it a break. Life isn't that bad.'

'What do you mean life isn't that bad?' I replied. 'I am over 40 and living with my parents. Every night I have to come home from work and listen to them bang on about what a complete balls-up I have made of my life. I have to eat fucking kippers for tea and I can't even turn the stereo up without being moaned at.'

'At least your mum's not dying of cancer,' Dave said.

He wasn't joking. Dave's mum has apparently got less than six months to live. She has been ill for a while but I didn't realise it was quite that bad.

I used to go to Dave's house after school. His family were richer than ours. They got a video and a computer before us and Dave and I would play Chuckie Egg or Elite until his mum called us down for tea. They ate earlier than we did, so sometimes I would eat with them and then go home and get fed again by my mum. I went on holiday to North Wales with them a couple of times too.

'I'm sorry Dave,' I said, feeling like a right arse for monopolising the conversation all night. We left the pub before last orders and I came home with a real determination to stop being so introspective, to stop being such a miserable twat. To start treating my parents better than I have been.

Wednesday 23rd April

Dave's news about his mum has really got to me. It has reminded me that life is finite. If you don't live it while you can, it has a habit of stopping at some point.

I have woken up today determined to cultivate a new, more positive attitude to life. I am renewing my focus on achieving my goals. I have only got five months to go until my birthday bash. I haven't achieved much so far by way of progress. I have probably drunk more in the last month than I have since I was a student. I have had the grand total of exactly three conversations with women who aren't either my ex or my mum, and I have done absolutely nothing to get a new job or a place of my own to live in. My kids and I are getting on OK but there is still a long way to go before I can confidently claim to have cracked the full-time dad with part-time access situation.

In my quest to be more positive, I phoned Andy and persuaded him to come out for a beer. This may have been my second night in the Morden Brook in the last three nights but I had an ulterior motive that, in my mind at least, outweighs the added alcohol consumption.

I am taking my dad's advice and am trying to find a hobby. Andy has got some interesting hobbies. Living on his own, he has to find something to do with his time I suppose.

Andy loves growing his own vegetables and spends half his life on his allotment. A couple of times a year he goes on weekend cookery courses, presumably to discover new and interesting things to do with his vegetables. He also paints. Believe it or not, he paints pictures of his vegetables.

'Aren't those hobbies a bit solitary?' I asked him.

'I guess they are, but the point is that I enjoy doing them,' he told me.

When Andy went up to get the next round in, I thought about his hobbies. Vegetable growing isn't for me. I can just about cope with eating cabbage or a marrow or broad beans but spending hours crawling around amongst the worms and the mud trying to coax the vegetables to grow isn't my scene. And as for painting, as any dad does, I gave it a go with my kids when they were young but that's as far as it goes. I definitely wasn't present when they were handing out the art genes.

So what do I like doing? I drew up a mental list:
1. Drinking with my mates
2. Playing golf – I haven't played for ages
3. Er. Not sure.

I played a bit of cricket in my youth. I thought about adding that to the list but cricket would eat into parts of my weekend that I try to keep free for seeing Jack and Sean. And besides, between you and me, a hobby that brings me into contact with women would be especially welcomed.

I turned to Andy for inspiration.

'If it's meeting women you want, then take up knitting,' he suggested.

When I was less than enthusiastic about his knitting idea (I want to meet pre-menopausal women, not someone's grandmother), Andy turned to the table of rather inebriated young lads sitting behind us and asked for their suggestions for a hobby for his newly divorced mate. Their suggestions ranged from wanking to glass-blowing (a bit random), from bowls to playing bridge or other things that old people do. Thanks lads, really useful.

Andy and I did at least arrange to play golf on Friday. I texted Dave and invited him too. I hope he can make it.

When I got home after pub chucking out time, I got more grief from my parents. They are feeling like 'glorified dog-sitters'. Is this the first step towards having to give Albus to my ex too? I wonder. I didn't rise to the bait though. In my newly found positive mindset, I offered to treat them to a meal out to thank them for looking after me and my dog over the last few months.

Friday 25th April

I took my parents to dinner in a little family-run Italian restaurant in Morden last night. With Frank Sinatra crooning away in the background and steam from our liqueur coffees rising gently in to the ether, I told my parents about Dave's news and my resulting positivity push.

'Does that mean you are going to try to unite your family under one roof again?' mum asked with genuine hope in her voice.

'No mum,' I told her, 'it just means I am sorry I have been an ungrateful git over the past few months and I will try harder in future to appreciate the things that you and dad are doing for me.'

As I was paying the bill I told my parents of my intention to go and play golf with Dave and Andy today.

'So I suppose we are left looking after your dog again while you swan around having a good time,' my dad moaned.

'Yes, but I am taking you up on your idea of getting a hobby, dad.' That seemed to pacify him a bit.

So today I picked up my golf clubs from my ex's garage and headed off in to the Surrey countryside to play golf.

Much to my ex's chagrin I used to play a fair bit of golf. When things weren't great at home I would escape to the sanctuary of the golf course and hit some balls, sometimes with Andy but at other times with the kids. The kids loved it for a year or two. They got to see their dad let his hair down (meaning they got to see me swear when I cocked a shot up). They tended to get chips too on the way home, which helped persuade them to come again.

Last year I even took my now ex to golf on one fateful occasion. Our marriage guidance counsellor recommended that we (me and my wife, not me and the counsellor; god, I feel ill just thinking about that option) got a shared hobby. Like most of our marriage guidance counsellor's theories, this idea was built on failed logic. It assumed we actually wanted to spend time together.

I persuaded my ex to try golf because in my mind at least that was preferable to me having to go horse-riding, her hobby of choice. To make the experience bearable for her I booked an overnight family suite at a golfing hotel with a spa in Sussex. We 'made love' the evening we arrived with reconciliation in mind (I may have had Kylie Minogue in mind but let's not go there).

The following morning we were warming up on the driving range before an introductory family golf lesson. My then wife repeatedly missed the ball off the tee with her eight iron.

'God mum, you're rubbish,' Sean said in that blunt way that only kids can get away with.

He walked up behind her to show her how to hold the club but she didn't see him coming and went for another big swing. At the height of her backswing she connected with Sean's nose. Instead of strolling through the Sussex countryside hitting a few balls, we spent the afternoon strolling through the Royal Sussex County hospital trying to find the casualty department.

Jack didn't help the family mood when he pointed out on the way home that Sean's nose was the only thing my ex had hit all day.

Anyway, back to today. Dave has a lot in common with Tiger Woods. Unfortunately for him, golf isn't one of those things. The saying 'all the gear but no idea' was written to describe Dave on the golf course. He looks good in his Ian Poulter (or should that be Rupert the Bear) trousers, but the image is ruined whenever he plays a shot. He's only just better than my ex.

Luckily for Dave, he didn't actually play a shot today. We met up in the clubhouse for a pre-round bacon sandwich and Dave got talking to an attractive woman in the shortest and possibly tightest golf shorts you have ever seen. After hanging around for half an hour waiting for him to finish telling big Bertha about the range on his wood, we left them to it and our threesome became two twosomes. I got a text mid-way through our round from Dave.

'Mark me down for a birdie at the 19th.' His mum being ill obviously wasn't putting Dave off his stride.

How come Dave finds it so easy to meet women? Andy isn't a stud like Dave but he has a certain quiet confidence that seems to attract women to him too. I asked him what I was doing wrong as we were walking through the rough on the second hole, trying to locate my ball.

'With you it's a confidence thing,' Andy told me. 'When I watched you in that night club the other night, you started physically sweating every time a woman so much as glanced in your direction. Why do you think that was?'

Astute observation. Good question. 'Because it was hot,' I said unconvincingly.

'Are you sure you are ready to meet someone? You are not long divorced,' Andy pointed out.

'Yes, I'm ready,' I replied, feeling pleased that Andy had asked a question I could answer for a change.

'You may be physically ready but are you mentally ready?' my friend-come-amateur psychologist observed. 'Is your awkwardness around women a result of you still feeling the scars of your marriage?'

And there was me thinking I was coming to play golf to get away from my troubles. Without overdoing the naval-gazing, Andy could have a point there though.

After living with my ex for fifteen years, some of my nervousness around women probably emanates from my not being used to women who are interested in what I have to say. As a consequence, to make a woman take notice of what I have to say, I have probably been trying too hard to make a real impact. Basically, I have been talking shit in the hope that a woman will listen to me.

Andy agreed. 'Just be yourself more. If a woman doesn't want to know when you are being yourself then you know she isn't the right woman,' he advised. 'Just be yourself and let fate take its course. If you are meant to meet someone then you will meet someone. Don't force the issue,' he added.

All I can say to that is that fate had better hurry up as it has been a while.

Andy and I had a good day. He thrashed the pants off me, but despite losing I managed to forget my troubles for a few holes at least. I would even go as far as to say that I felt like a participating member of society rather than a divorced man for a couple of hours.

Saturday 26th April

In keeping with my new-found proactive state, I have taken my first steps towards finding somewhere to live. I registered with some local estate agents.

I have also decided that I am going to take the children on holiday in the summer. Dave's mum's illness has made me realise that life is too short to waste. The three of us would really benefit from having a good holiday. We all deserve it.

How am I going to afford these extravagances? I have actually managed to squirrel a few quid away over the past couple of months, but don't tell my ex. I was saving it for a rainy day but now seems like as good a time as any to break in to it.

We went into Thomas Cook to have a look through a few brochures. I was thinking along the lines of the Isle of Wight. But as the morning progressed, the spec seemed to grow with the kids uttering phrases like 'It has to be sunny', 'we have to have a swimming pool', 'it would be cool to be near a theme park', 'and a water park', 'a swim-up pool bar' (OK, that was mine), 'the Med not some cold sea', and 'they must do pizza'. Eventually I told the kids I got the idea and we agreed that I would book something. The mere fact that they got excited about the thought of going on holiday with me made my day.

My mum and dad have gone to Eastbourne for the week-end so we had their house to ourselves. I took the opportunity to get in to their kitchen and dust off my culinary skills. I made the kids some home-made burgers and potato wedges with a home-made tomato salsa. I thought it was a pretty decent meal.

Sean disagreed. 'I would have preferred a McDonald's,' was his considered verdict.

Sunday 27th April

After a quick chat with Dave I decided to pay his mum a visit this morning. She was good to me when I was younger, so I wanted to at least let her know I was thinking about her.

I knocked on Dave's parents' door with the prerequisite bunch of flowers in my hand.

'Thanks for the flowers,' Mrs Fazackerley said once Dave's dad had shown me into the living room.

When I was growing up I felt a bit starstruck when I was in a room with Dave's mum and dad. Both of them were renowned musicians and great raconteurs and they loved to play to us and tell us stories of life in the 60s. Dave and I would play with them too, him on the keyboards and me on the drums. I had no talent but I would give them a bash and try and pretend that I knew what I was doing.

Seeing Mrs F today though, I found it hard to believe that this was the same woman who had filled a room with the sound of her saxophone. She was sitting in her favourite chair by the window with a blanket wrapped around her legs. It took me a second to get over how frail she looked. She had always taken great pride in her appearance, but no amount of make-up or expensive clothing could hide the pallor of her skin.

'You've just picked these up from the cemetery, haven't you?' she asked me, holding out the flowers.

'Yes,' I acknowledged sheepishly. Not literally off someone's grave but from the flower seller who sets up a stall outside the cemetery gates on Sundays and religious holidays. 'How could you tell?'

'Because they smell of death. I am not dead yet, you know,' Mrs F pointed out with a wry smile and a glint in her eye as she passed the flowers to Dave's dad.

I apologised for the insensitivity of my purchase but she dismissed the matter with a wave of her hand.

'How are you doing?' she asked me.

Rather than giving her the glib response I so often seem to come up with when people ask me that question these days, I was fairly honest with Mrs F.

'Oh, you know, I am trying my best to come to terms with being single and being a distant dad.'

'So I hear,' she responded. 'But you're lucky. You are young enough to start again. Imagine what that miserable old git is going to do when I die.' She gestured to Dave's dad who was searching through the dresser for an appropriate sized vase for the flowers.

'I'm going to have a party,' he said without turning around.

'You are a good man, Graham. You will find someone that is right for you,' she predicted, ignoring her husband.

When Dave's dad eventually found the right vase and headed for the kitchen to sort the flowers out, Dave's mum noticeably made an effort to sit up. She gestured for me to come and sit next to her.

'Graham, will you make this dying woman one promise?' When I nodded, she went on, 'When I have gone, Dave is going to need your help. Will you promise me you will stand by him and be there when he needs you?'

'Of course I will,' I responded. 'That's what friends are for after all.'

'I am not going to go in to the details but I am not just talking about helping him grieve,' she continued. 'There'll be a lot on his mind when I have gone. He's going to find a few things out that will surprise him. You need to be there for him.'

Becoming a little bit curious now, I repeated my assurance that I will be there for Dave. Just as Mr F was coming back into the room with the worst flower arrangement I had ever seen, Dave's mum made me promise that I wouldn't ever mention this part of our conversation to Dave.

I haven't got a clue what she could have been talking about, but I will be there for Dave if and when he needs me.

I went back to my parents' house doubly determined to sort my life out while I still can.

Monday 28th April

After work this evening I looked at a couple of properties. I had some real dilemmas about where to live. I need to find somewhere that is convenient for the kids – fairly near to their school, their friends and their various sports clubs. The more convenient the location, the more often they are likely to call in. But on the other hand I don't want to be too near to the ex. Although there isn't that much animosity between us most of the time, I don't want to meet her when buying my groceries at the Co-op or, worse still, my condoms at the chemist. Still, none of this may be too much of an issue if she ups sticks and moves to Exeter.

I settled on looking at properties in Morden.

The rents of the places I looked at tonight were nearly half my salary. I am still paying a quarter of my salary to my ex to fund the mortgage on 'her' house and the upkeep of the kids. Which would leave me a quarter of my salary to live on. That would mean that on Mondays, Tuesdays and Wednesday mornings I would be working to pay rent; Wednesday lunchtime through to my mid-afternoon tea on Thursday I would be working to fund my ex's current life; and for the rest of the week I will be working to fund my new life. Best not to dwell on this, I reckon.

The first flat I looked at didn't look too bad. In estate

agent language, the rooms were well apportioned, the flat had a south-facing aspect and all mod cons. Unfortunately it also had a sex-mad couple living in the flat directly above. If I could hear their grinding and groaning at six o'clock in the evening, imagine what noises they would be making after a few drinks on a Friday night. With me in the middle of the longest barren spell of my adult life, those sounds would very quickly drive me insane. As the noise from upstairs reached its climax, even the estate agent gave up trying to tell me the flat would support a lifestyle of domestic bliss.

I knew the second flat was a no-hoper the moment I saw it from the outside. It was in a large block with staircases that reeked of piss and external corridors littered with abandoned sofas or bikes with their wheels missing. The graffiti-covered walls included words that I wouldn't want my fairly broad-minded children to see. I didn't even bother going inside.

Call me a snob if you like but I told the estate agent in no uncertain terms that I wouldn't allow my kids to grow up in a piss-infested hell-hole. He promised to re-evaluate the list of properties he was planning to show me later in the week and we just about parted on civil terms.

Wednesday 30th April

Today was a red letter day in my post-divorce life. No, I didn't have sex, but I did go out for a drink with a woman. And not a mum of a friend of the children either. I took Julia, aka Miss Putney, to the Wetherspoons pub in Wimbledon. I know it is not the top of Eiffel Tower or even an attractive bar on the Thames, but it was convenient for both of us.

Despite me definitely being 'over' my ex, part of me was half-hoping that someone my ex knows would see me and Julia out together in Wimbledon and report back. We didn't see a soul we knew all night.

I don't think I would be doing her a disservice when I say that if there was a Miss Putney contest, Julia wouldn't win it. Nevertheless, she is a perfectly presentable, well turned out woman with curves in the right places. She may well be having a hairstyle crisis though because her mullet has been chopped off and she now has short, spiky hair. She looks a bit severe but when she smiles, her whole face lights up. I kept wanting to, but in the end I didn't dare ask her about her hair.

Julia is a civil servant working in the Home Office. She didn't tell me exactly what she did, I suspect more because it is boring than because she is sworn to secrecy, but who knows, she might be some sort of spy. She hasn't been married before, but she has fairly recently split from a long-term partner. She doesn't have any kids of her own but she managed to muster up an appropriate level of interest when I talked about Jack and Sean.

The drink graduated into dinner. She went for fish and chips, I went for burger, which I regretted when burger juice started dripping down my chin.

We chatted warmly but again for the life of me I can't remember what about. I wasn't too nervous and for once in my life I didn't make a fool of myself. We may meet up again, unless I misread the signs, which is entirely possible due to my lack of recent experience in this area.

Saturday 3rd May

Jack is off at a cadets' trek in the Brecon Beacons this weekend so I spent the day with Sean.

Sean and I had a chill-out. We watched 'Back to the Future' on DVD and ate too much junk food. Don't mention the 'getting fit' thing. After the film, Sean asked me what I would do if I could travel through time.

'I don't know, maybe go back to 1966 and watch England win the World Cup. Or to 1969 and watch Neil Armstrong take his first steps on the moon.'

'Wouldn't you go back to all the times you were horrible to mum and change them?' my son asked me.

I kicked myself for not realising it was a serious question. If I was living that part of my life again, I am still not sure I could change things too much for the better. Everyone does things wrong. I could certainly have been nicer to my wife at times. I could have done less drinking with my mates. I could have told the truth about knocking the garden wall down when reversing the car out of the drive. I could have made more effort to show an interest in her and her passions. A few different responses here and there might have prolonged our relationship a bit, but I really don't think it would have changed anything in the long run.

After considering my response to Sean's question for a

while I chose to duck it by asking him whether that is what he would do.

'Yes. I would go back to all those times where she told me to tidy my bedroom and I didn't do it and I would tidy it. And do you remember when I dropped my whole glass of milk on the sofa and didn't tell anyone?'

'I remember.' I grimaced. We had gone on holiday that day and when we got back two weeks later the house absolutely stank of stale milk.

'Well, I would go back in time and put that right,' Sean told me. 'Do you think we would all still live in the same house if I did that?'

This was the first time that one of my boys had asked me, albeit indirectly, whether they shared any of the blame for our divorce. My kids never think they are to blame for anything. Ever. So I was surprised when Sean brought the subject up today.

I did my best to reassure him.

'Sean, you know the tidy bedroom thing wasn't anything to do with why your mum and me split up. And nor was you spilling milk on the sofa. Mum blamed me for that anyway, not you. The reason we split up was because we had nothing in common in our lives other than you and Jack. When we weren't talking about you, we had nothing good to say to each other. That's why we split up.'

'Then why didn't you just talk about us all the time?' Sean asked.

Luckily, mine and Sean's conversation was interrupted by a phone call. Totally out of the blue, Bryan Green (he of the dinner party) phoned and asked if the boys and I fancied coming on holiday with them. The Greens were supposed to be going with Katie's sister's family, the Browns (honestly) but the Browns have had to pull out because Katie's sister has just realised she is five months pregnant (honestly again). They had booked a villa in Turkey large enough to accommodate eight people and are now keen not to have to foot the whole bill themselves.

The holiday isn't too expensive so I jumped at the chance of the Hopes coming off the substitutes' bench and replacing the Browns. I am quite chuffed with this result as both families get along well. Jack and Sean will particularly enjoy having Josh and Theo, Katie and Bryan's kids, to hang out with.

Sunday 4th May

In my pursuit of my ongoing quest to get a life I browsed through the large selection of self-help books on the shelves of my local bookshop after dropping Sean off at his mum's. They all sounded a load of old bollocks to me. I reckon they should do an experiment. The next time two identical twins are born, make one read one self-help book a month for the whole of his life and don't let the other read any. Then, on their 60th birthday, ask them who has had the best life. I bet it would be the one who didn't spend half his life reading that self-righteous claptrap.

When I was in the bookshop I saw our marriage guidance counsellor browsing in the 'travel' section.

'Thinking of going somewhere?' I asked her.

'I am just looking really,' she replied, struggling to find me in her memory bank.

I introduced myself and a light went on in her eyes as she remembered me. She tried to scarper.

'Shouldn't you be in the 'health and fitness' section?' I hollered at her back as she hurried out of the shop. She is the largest woman I have ever met. I got some dirty looks from my fellow shoppers but that bit of cruelty at my counsellor's expense made me feel good.

As well as her being rather large, there are a couple of

other things you should know about our marriage guidance counsellor. She has got a moustache that rivals Daley Thompson's and Merv Hughes's and, probably not unconnected, she has never been married. I found it hard to take advice on saving my marriage from a person who has no actual experience of the concept.

I am surprised she couldn't place me straight away today. The last time we met was pretty memorable.

In our first session we had covered things like how much time my then wife and I spent talking to each other (none), our relationships with our parents (fine), our relationships with each other's parents (hers with mine fine, mine with hers anything but fine), our hobbies (fine until she suggested my wife went with me) and our approach to parenthood (not bad). In the second – and as it turned out, last – session, we talked about our sex life.

'When was the last time you made love?'

'Last week,' I replied.

'I can't remember,' my wife said.

'Do you engage in foreplay before sex?'

'Yes,' from me.

'No,' from my ex. Are we talking about the same sex?

'Do you reach climax in your love-making?'

A 'Yes' from me.

A 'No' from my ex.

'Is your sex loving and sensual or a routine you go through because you think you should?' our relationship 'expert' asked.

My wife went for 'routine'. I went for the therapist. 'What's the point of dissecting our sex life like this? Isn't it bloody obvious we hardly ever shag? We wouldn't have come to see you if we did it every night, would we? Do you get off on watching other people talk about their sex lives? I bet you've never even had sex, have you? Have you ever been touched? Have you ever had an orgasm? Go on, tell us. We've got a right to know who we're working with here.'

At which point I was asked to leave. To my ex's credit, she laughed and left with me. We actually had pretty good sex that night too, with foreplay and orgasms and everything.

Tuesday 6th May

Today's good news is that we are having a 'strategic review' at work. I didn't have a clue what a strategic review was so I asked my boss Daniel ('Don't call me Dan, my name is Daniel'). Apparently it means they look at the purpose of the organisation, refine and narrow it, and then see what human resources they need to deliver it. I didn't know what that meant either so I gave up trying to understand it.

Thursday 8th May

My ex phoned me today to tell me that her dad has got worse, she is going off to Exeter for a couple of days to be with him and would I have the kids? The best thing about my divorce was that my father-in-law became my ex-father-in-law. I suppose I wouldn't wish illness on anyone, but if it gets me more time with the children then so be it. And the kids' school is closed for teacher training too, so good news nearly all round.

I have booked tomorrow off work and the three of us are going to go camping.

My ex was never one for sleeping under canvas. She needed her home comforts and particularly couldn't stand having to walk to the toilet block. We did try camping once. We went to a campsite by the sea in Devon. After a four hour drive in steaming hot sunshine, the heavens opened the minute we arrived at the camp site. We got soaked and had a row over how to put the tent up.

The kids were young on that trip. The first and only morning we were there, the boys woke up at half past three and wouldn't go back to sleep. They were told in no uncertain terms to shut up. Five minutes later they were chatting again. My then wife told them that if they didn't shut up until at least six o'clock we would go straight home.

They were too excited about the adventures that lay ahead. Within ten minutes they were talking again so their mum made me get up, pack our things back up and drive home. Needless to say, I didn't bother suggesting we go camping again as a family.

The boys have been camping several times since that experience. They go regularly with scouts and cadets. In fact it was Jack who suggested the camp site that I have just booked, in Swanage, Dorset.

Jack is well up for our trip. He loves the outdoors and can't wait for the challenge of building a fire and cooking sausages over it. Sean took a bit more convincing though.

'Can I take my PS4 with me?' he asked as we were packing the car.

'There won't be anywhere to plug it in when we get there,' I pointed out.

'I wish I had gone to Exeter with mum,' he said, somewhat sulkily.

I am going to make it my mission over the next few days to have a great time with the boys.

Sunday 11ᵗʰ May

I am feeling quite pleased with myself. Our boys' weekend in Dorset went well. Even Sean had a good time despite not seeing hide nor hair of a computer screen for four days.

The weekend wasn't without its trials and tribulations though. We took the dog with us but I hadn't thought to check whether dogs were allowed at the campsite. The prominent 'Strictly No Dogs' sign at the side of the road alerted us to our error. Jack put his coat over Albus, who was laying down in the boot, as we were let through the security gate and into the campsite.

The site was pretty primitive. It consisted of a large sloping field and a toilet block. There were only a couple of other tents up when we arrived. Because we had the dog we chose a position in the furthest corner of the field, as far away from the other campers as we could get.

At Jack's insistence I let the boys put the tent up. They did a great job of it. Jack might only be fourteen but he is already more practical-minded and good with his hands than me. Sean was his willing assistant, content to take orders from his older brother.

While the kids were bashing the last few tent pegs in to the ground, I nipped down the road and bought us all fish and chips for dinner. We sat on the grass and were eating happily until Jack hit on a thought. We hadn't packed the dog's food. I bet you can tell who used to do the packing in our household. Off I trotted back to the chip shop.

'Large cod and chips for the German Shepherd please.'

We had a decent night's sleep on that first night. The following morning, after a breakfast of bacon sandwiches for four, we went for a long walk over the Purbeck hills. The views were spectacular.

Albus spent hours barking at sheep and chasing the boys. My ex and I had bought the dog in an effort to create days like this. It is a shame she wasn't there with us to enjoy it. I do still miss her sometimes. She would have put Albus on his lead to stop him chasing sheep, she would have brought the dog food with her rather than buying him a half-pound burger for lunch and she would definitely not have let him lick my ice cream when I wasn't looking, as Sean did. But despite being the sensible one, she would have added something to the day.

When we returned to the campsite, it was jam-packed. Half the world seemed to have decided to converge on our corner of the Dorset countryside. They were there for a kite festival. Until this weekend I had thought that kites were things that kids younger than mine played with for five minutes before they got tangled up or stuck in a tree. Apparently I was wrong. Kites of all shapes and sizes were laid out over cars and on every spare inch of grass. People were admiring each other's babies. It was quite funny to watch.

The other thing that made the boys laugh was that we now weren't the only ones to have smuggled a dog in to the campsite. As we were busy cooking our sausages for dinner, Albus was chasing his new BFF around the neighbouring field.

Yesterday we hit the beach. We thought we had better find somewhere off the beaten track because we didn't want the dog to keep running off with little Bobby's football or Angel's sandwich (he has got a taste for sandwiches now) so we drove to Studland Bay, a less well-populated beach than Swanage.

I hadn't known in advance but I chuckled to myself when I saw the 'naturists beyond this point' sign as we were walking to the beach.

We were the first ones on the beach and had an hour of fun trying to entice the dog into the sea. Gradually, though, other people started arriving. It was only a matter of time.

I was digging a hole with the boys and the dog when a shocked look suddenly appeared on Jack's face.

'Dad, that man's got no swimming trunks on,' he exclaimed.

'Son, didn't you see the signs?' I asked him.

'What signs?' Jack queried.

'The ones that said 'naturists beyond this point',' I enlightened him.

'I did but I thought it meant bird spotters or something boring like that, not naked people,' Jack said.

My boys are at either ends of the spectrum when it comes to their attitudes to nudity. Sean will parade around the house naked and proud, whereas Jack won't even get changed in front of his brother. Jack literally got into the hole we were digging and refused to come out. Sean and I got naked and ran in to the sea laughing.

We finished the day off with a pub tea (the kids wanted to buy Albus a steak but I thought sausages in onion gravy was a better option).

'Thanks, dad, we've had a great time,' Jack said as he was polishing off his last mouthful.

It was a shame to have to come back home so soon. Especially as the first thing I did when I got back was have another row with my ex.

When I dropped the kids back at her house, she told me her dad wasn't doing very well at all. She was now even more seriously thinking about moving to Exeter. I didn't learn from the mistakes I made the last time we had this conversation. In fact I repeated them pretty much verbatim.

'You wouldn't want to miss out on your dad's twilight years, would you,' I agreed. 'Go to Exeter. I promise I will bring the kids to see you at least once a month.'

'You're a twat, Graham. I hate you,' she shouted as she slammed the door in my face.

I wasn't particularly proud of myself for that remark. If my dad was ill, the last thing I would want is my ex taunting me. I had only got out of her drive when I decided I should go back and apologise. I turned the car around and knocked on the door.

'I am sorry, that was uncalled for,' I told her when she answered.

'Just fuck off Graham,' she said and slammed the door again.

I know I can be a dick at times. My glib remarks have quite often got me into trouble. If it's any consolation though, I am not bad at apologising when I am wrong. My ex never apologises for anything. She is never wrong. And she is probably going to take my kids to Exeter. Why is it that she has all the power when it comes to making decisions about the children?

Tuesday 13th May

Tonight I enjoyed another evening out with Julia. You may note that I am not referring to it as a 'date'. Do middle-aged people date or do they just fall into polite companionship? I hope they can date, but my times with Julia feel more like companionship. They feel completely different from the first few times I met up with my ex. With my ex I just wanted to touch her, to kiss her. I dreaded that point in the evening when it would be time to say goodbye. With Julia, I am not experiencing any of those feelings. There isn't a spark there, no lust. But I do enjoy Julia's company and it makes a pleasant change from spending the evenings with my parents or my blokey mates down the pub.

I am not sure whether Julia fancies me or not. I am rubbish at telling whether women like me. Maybe it is because not many do so I haven't had much practice in seeing the signs. Even when I was younger, in my pre-married life, I could never read the signs. A strong fear of rejection kept me in check. I would often be told by girlfriends once relationships had been consummated that I could have moved from the 'flirting' phase to the 'action' phase a lot quicker than I had. Thinking about it, most of my girlfriends kissed me first rather than me making the first move. My ex stuck her tongue down my throat at the end of our first meal out, at the Barley Mow in Horseferry Road.

Even though there was no spark there, I thought about kissing Julia tonight. It would have at least shown me whether or not she fancies me. I would like to think she does. It would be nice to have some affirmation that I am actually an eligible single bloke.

Instead of kissing Julia, at the end of our Thai meal in Wimbledon Village, we smiled at each other and went our separate ways.

Wednesday 14th May

My 'get somewhere to live' goal came a big step closer to being achieved today, but not in a way I had anticipated. Andy emailed me to say that his work have asked him to head up their new office in Toronto. Until today I thought he was just an office manager – the man who buys the staples and hires the cleaners. But he is obviously more than that, unless Canada is lacking in staple-buyers.

Anyway, Andy has a two-bed maisonette in St Helier. That's the south west London St Helier rather than the one in Jersey. Knowing that I am trying to move out of my parents' house as soon as possible, Andy asked me if I fancied renting his flat out for a year while he is away. It is a decent flat and even has a garden. It maybe isn't quite where I would have chosen to locate myself in an ideal world, but Andy will do me a good deal on the rent and it will mean I don't have to listen to any more inane bollocks from estate agents.

I am minded to take Andy up on his offer. I will talk to Jack and Sean first though.

Although his flat might be a godsend, I will miss Andy's company. He is the boring one but if truth be told, I probably have more in common with Andy than with most of my other mates. He likes his sport, he follows the news and isn't frightened to get off his backside to do something different from time to time. Like relocate to Canada. The only thing I don't have in common with Andy is his taste in music. If I do move in to his flat, I need to make sure he takes his Jean Michel Jarre electronic pop or whatever it is called CDs with him.

Saturday 17th May

Jack and Sean seem a bit less excited about me moving in to Andy's flat than I am. They are concerned about the location. The fact that it may be in a crime hotspot on the middle of a once-notorious estate doesn't bother them. It is just that it is a bit of a trek from their school and it isn't 'on the way' to anywhere. My parents' is on the way to their mum's from school so they do drop in there sometimes unannounced and on a whim – even after the kipper incident. I guess I am going to have to politely decline Andy's offer. Back to the drawing board, I suppose.

I tried to help Sean with his homework tonight. His English teacher asked his class to write a short story using lots of descriptive writing.

'What's your story going to be about?' I asked him.

'It's about a family whose parents don't like each other anymore,' Sean told me matter of factly.

Once he had written his story, he let me read it. He has written about the two parents splitting up and the children living with each parent for part of the week. The gist of Sean's story is that the children are happier because their parents are happier. The other angle to Sean's story is that the two boys help each other through the hard times and are closer than they used to be as a result. The big brother does still smell though.

'Is this how you feel?' I asked Sean after finishing reading the story.

'No, it's not about me dad. Mrs Pearce said it had to be made up,' Sean explained.

My boy has a good imagination but I am not sure it is that good. I like to think that there was at least an element of truth in his writing. In fact I got a bit emotional when I read it. Even though he said it was made up, I gave him a cuddle and ruffled his hair.

Monday 19th May

The boys and I are going to Turkey in about two months' time. Yesterday, a little voice inside my head told me to check Jack and Sean's passports. Lo and behold, Sean's runs out the day before we are due to fly.

So today I went to the post office at lunchtime to renew it. I filled in the forms surreptitiously at work this afternoon and took them back to the post office. I paid extra for the woman behind the counter to check my form and send it off as I have been known to cock forms up. I wish I hadn't bothered paying the extra.

The clerk tried to tell me that Sean's mother had to fill in the form, not me.

'What if she's dead?' I asked.

'Is she?' the woman replied.

'No,' I was forced to admit.

'Well, then she has to sign the application,' the officious jobsworth pronounced.

I am sure she thought she was striking a significant blow for women's lib. I got stroppy and told her I wanted to see the specific clause that prohibits a dad from signing his son's passport renewal form. She couldn't find it so on my insistence she phoned her head office who eventually told her that she was talking out of her arse. When she stamped the form I smiled. Dads one, post office woman nil.

Tuesday 20th May

I met the 'your dog weed on my dog's head' woman again this evening during a walk on Wimbledon Common. She remembered me. Well, I suspect she remembered Albus more. Albus is about ten times the size of her dog, but that didn't stop him trying to have sex with her. Again, I wish I had some of his self-confidence.

The lovely dog-walking woman and I chatted for a while and I even managed not to mention my divorce or my kids. I asked her about her strange looking dog. Apparently it is a shih poo (she pronounced it shit poo) – a cross between a shih tzu and a poodle. I suppose it would have been worse if a bulldog had mated with a shih tzu.

Actually, I couldn't have embarrassed myself too much because at the end of our walk, she suggested that we meet at the same time next week. I went to bed with a smile on my face despite not even knowing her name.

Wednesday 21st May

The world cup starts in less than a month. Our work's head office decided it would be good for morale if they organised an evening of inter-office football. I am not sure why, but people at work do seem miserable at the moment. Even more miserable than usual, I mean.

The powers that be decided on a sales-versus-back-office match. There is always a bit of good-natured banter between the sales show-offs and the back-office boys. As my boss wouldn't let me within a mile of an actual customer, I am firmly in the back office camp, or the engine room of the company as we like to think of it.

Now I used to fancy myself as a half-decent left-back. When playing on the school fields of south west London I modelled my game on that of my hero, 'psycho' Stuart Pearce. In my heyday (I am not sure whether a very short spell of being slightly less crap than I normally am constitutes a heyday but we won't dwell on that question) opposition strikers would have probably described me as a dirty bastard. I preferred the term 'swashbuckling'.

I was quite chuffed when Daniel, my boss and the back-office team's player manager, included me on his team sheet. The team was published yesterday on the work intranet. We all turned up at Regent's Park eagerly anticipating a hard-fought contest.

After a rousing team talk from Daniel (more David Brent than Jose Mourinho), the match kicked off. Now although I would love to be a football reporter, I will resist the urge to practise by giving a blow-by-blow account of the game. Suffice it to say that stock phrases such as 'men against boys', 'shocking defending' and 'couldn't hit a barn door' would all feature. I could add in 'it's a game of two halves' but unfortunately in this case, the two halves were the same. In short, the back-office boys were thrashed by the sales team. Flash Harry and fancy Dan both scored hat-tricks.

I should confess to one incident that occurred during the game. When the score was still goalless, I picked up the ball from our goalie 'fatboy Tim' and went on a dazzling run, right through the heart of their midfield, veering one way and another, carrying the ball right up to the edge of the sales penalty area. It was Maradona-esque up to this point. With only one defender left to beat and with a teammate unmarked in the middle in acres of space, I chose to shoot. Big mistake. Not just because the ball sailed way over the bar but more importantly because the teammate I should have passed to was Daniel, my boss. There goes any chance of my bonus this year.

In the bar afterwards, my team-mates christened me 'Notta Hope'. I first heard this nickname some thirty years ago but I didn't let on. Calling them unoriginal would have just rubbed salt in wounds I had already opened.

Thursday 22nd May

The work 'strategic review' report was published today. I have now realised what all that gobbledygook management-speak Daniel came out with meant. It meant they sack a few people to save money. They probably deliberately waited until after the football so as to avoid lots of career-ending tackles flying about. And I didn't pass to Daniel. It should have been my job I worried about losing, not just my bonus.

Apparently instead of the current two logistics managers, in the future they only need one.

They are running a consultation on their proposals, so, as one of the affected logistics managers, I submitted a considered response telling them that I didn't think the proposals were any good. I am not optimistic that my submission will sway their thinking.

Short skirt Sarah, who noticed the absence of my wedding ring a few weeks ago, is the other logistics manager. It looks like the two of us will have to compete for one job. Sarah is always in the office before me in the mornings and shows no sign of leaving when I am getting my coat on in the evenings. She is an attractive woman who, even before having to compete for her job, was very pally with Daniel. This is going to be a close fight then.

With the prospect of losing my job now a distinct possibility, maybe now isn't the time I should be looking to move out of my parents' house. Maybe it isn't the time but I am still determined to press ahead and move out. I need to believe in myself. I will get that job. And if I don't get that one, I will get another job. Perhaps the strategic review is the catalyst that will force me into finding a newer, more interesting job.

Sunday 25th May

This is the first weekend I haven't seen my boys at all since the divorce. They have gone to Exeter with the ex. We used to go and visit her family a couple of times a year. Jack and Sean have never been particularly close to that set of grandparents but they trudged along compliantly with us. When I talked to them on the phone before they went, I got the impression that they were looking forward to this trip even less than usual.

'Granddad spends half his time moaning about you and the other half moaning at us,' Jack mumbled when I asked him why the extra reluctance to go. 'Just ignore him, he's a dickhead,' I told my son. No I didn't but I wanted to.

I am getting a real sense that the boys are beginning to find their feet again after a tricky time when their mum and I split up. Sean in particular seems to be coming out of his shell. I sensed on our recent camping trip that he seemed more upbeat, more relaxed. He told me to stop worrying about him when I asked him how he was. His exact words were, 'Stop worrying about me and start sorting your life out.' Cheeky git.

Like Sean, I am feeling a bit less insecure now than I was a couple of months ago. This isn't quite the same as saying I am 'a bit more secure' but it is a start at least.

Despite me not seeing the boys this weekend, I haven't spent the whole time moping about. I haven't been too downhearted. The boys and I continue to get on well. They seem to respect me and listen to me despite me not being there all the time and they do genuinely want to see me. Both boys periodically drop in at my parents' because they fancy a chat. They both want me to come to their various sports matches. They are both interested and engaged in my flat-finding endeavour too. If they had missed a whole weekend's visit a couple of months ago I would literally have spent the whole weekend worrying about what they were up to, but this weekend I managed to function without them.

Of course, my different mindset has nothing to do with my Tuesday evening dog walks.

I actually took a couple more tentative steps towards achieving some of my goals this weekend. I went on a long bike ride and I made a concerted effort to sort my living arrangements out.

I spent most of Saturday in the company of estate agents but other than that I didn't have a bad day. I may have found a flat with some prospects. It is off Martin Way in Morden. It is only a ten minute walk from school and on the way to my ex's, which means the kids could drop in when passing. It is also only five minutes from my parents' so I could go round there for dinner every so often, which might not be a bad thing because I may have forgotten how to cook since not owning my own kitchen. I will take the kids to view the flat sometime next week.

I thought a fair bit about my job too this weekend. It may be under threat but I am determined not to think of myself as a victim. I must not wallow. I must not wallow. I must not wallow. You see, who needs a stupid self-help book?

I do try to adhere to the philosophy that shit happens to those who let shit happen (not sure whether that one was Rousseau, Plato or Marx?). In other words, I am doing a boring job at the moment and some jerk in a suit may decide I'm surplus to requirements. I could sit there and passively let Daniel not Dan kick me out. Or I could take control of the situation and find myself a better job. I got online and started working on a few application forms.

On Saturday night I stayed in and dog-sat as my parents went out for dinner with friends. The thought of my nigh-on 70-year-old parents going out on a Saturday night and me staying in on my own would normally bring on a bout of depression, but instead I just enjoyed having the house to myself and being in control of the sound system. The Buddy Holly CD was firmly ejected from my parents' CD player in favour of a bit of Dire Straits.

Tuesday 27th May

When I drove through Raynes Park and up towards the Common this evening, I had little optimism that dog walking woman would show up. The weather was utterly awful. Albus and I got soaked just getting into the car. What self-respecting goddess would walk their dog in such shitty weather?

At this point I feel the need to make a confession. I have been looking forward to tonight since the moment I waved goodbye to dog-walking woman last week. And not just a little bit either. I have spent many a minute fantasising about us as a couple, eating dinner together, chatting over a drink and, yes, doing other things too. I haven't admitted it before now because it would have sounded a bit over the top, even a bit creepy. We have probably only exchanged about a hundred words with each other. I don't even know her name unless by some miraculous trick of fate her parents christened her dog-walking woman.

As I drove into the Windmill car park, my worst fears were confirmed. The car park was totally deserted. I was gutted. I sat in the car for a few minutes, firstly cursing the British weather and then beginning to wonder whether she would have shown up even if the sun had been out. She probably just decided I wasn't the stimulating, attractive, intelligent hunk I wanted her to think I was.

Eventually, Albus became impatient being stuck in the car with the windows steaming up, so, feeling disconsolate, I did my coat up and braved the rain.

This is where things get a bit messy. Albus plodded over towards the café and decided that the path outside the café was the best place on the whole Common to do his business. Like any responsible dog owner I carried what are colloquially known as 'poo bags' with me. I was in the process of picking up the biggest turd in history with a bag that wasn't man enough for the job when the shih poo and her lovely owner walked round the corner. This wasn't how I'd imagined our next encounter to start.

But start it had. 'Good to see you aren't frightened of getting your hands dirty,' dog-walking woman, who subsequently became known as Amy, said with a smile on her face that literally altered the rhythm of my heart.

'Good to see you aren't the sort of woman to let a little rain put you off a walk,' I replied. Not a bad opener.

Somehow, Amy managed to look stunning even though she was soaked to the skin and covered head to toe in expensive rain clothes that would probably have passed muster in the Amazon rainforest. My cheap 'waterproof' wouldn't have kept me dry in the Rainforest Café. She became known as Amy at about the point that I had dropped the foul smelling deposit off in the nearest dog bin.

We chatted away in the rain as we strolled across the Common. Amy lives off the Ridgway in Wimbledon Village. She is divorced and has one child, Lucy. Lucy is fourteen, the same age as Jack. She was with her dad this evening in Earlsfield. I am divorced, have two children, am in the process of sorting my living accommodation out et cetera, et cetera... Amy wants to be a travel writer when she grows up. I have tried growing up and it is thoroughly over-rated.

We might have talked about where we are going in life, but

we didn't discuss where we were going on our walk. We just kept walking in the rain and increasing darkness. We ended up walking past Cannizaro House and found ourselves outside the Crooked Billet pub. And then inside, with our soaking wet, tired dogs at our feet and Amy nursing a steaming hot cup of coffee and me a pint.

Once we had stripped our clothes off in a frantic manner (OK, only our waterproofs), I got a better look at Amy. She happens to be the opposite of my ex in a lot of ways – redhead with long wavy (slightly bedraggled tonight) hair versus dyed blonde bob; striking emerald green eyes versus nondescript brown; tall and leggy versus short and anything but; and with an electric smile that she isn't afraid to use rather than a permanent miserable frown. That just turned into an excuse for a rant but I am sure you get the picture.

I don't know why but the nerves that have characterised my interactions with women over the last few months weren't present tonight. Andy's advice to me on the golf course was just to be myself and I would be alright. I didn't try to come across as some sort of smartarse. I talked to Amy about relationships, about divorce and its impact upon us and the children. I held my end up in the conversation. I did OK.

There was no physical contact tonight. Was this because I still lack the killer instinct? Possibly. I said I wasn't nervous but that isn't the same as saying I am super cool, confident and cocksure. When all's said and done, that will never be me. I didn't even get her phone number but we did agree the standard 'same time next week' arrangement before we both got taxis home. My car is spending a solitary night in the Windmill car park which will mean another trip to the Common tomorrow night for me.

Wednesday 28th May

The consultation on the strategic review is still rumbling on. Daniel asked me about my domestic situation today and told me he hopes it isn't affecting my work. I wonder who told him about it. Probably the same person I saw going out to lunch with him. Short skirt Sarah.

Not unrelated to the above, I thought a bit more about my future career prospects. What sort of jobs should I be applying for? What would I like to do? I am an educated man. I would quite like a new challenge. As I have mentioned before, something like journalism appeals, particularly sports journalism. But realistically I am probably twenty years too old to start along that path. I would also love to work with animals, but other than liking animals and thinking that animals generally like me, I have no particular qualification that would make me appointable by zoos or vets. I also have a desire to work outdoors but I can't stand gardening, I am crap at putting a shelf up so I guess I wouldn't make a great builder and I don't even paint my own house so I don't think there is a career there either. I reckon after spending most of the last month with estate agents, I could probably do a better job than half of them. I am sure I could sell more properties simply by cutting out the bullshit and being honest.

What I would like to do and what I can realistically afford

to do are two different things. I can't afford to take a pay cut, which stops me from starting a new career as the wet-behind-the-ears new boy. So I dusted off my CV today and started looking at jobs that are vaguely related to my project management experience, problem-solving skills and organ-isational abilities. 'Organisational abilities' – what a load of nonsense. I am the sort of person who forgets appoint-ments, rarely remembers birthdays, never has any food in the fridge (when I used to have my own fridge) and books holiday villas but forgets to book the flights. But apparently I have 'well-developed organisational abilities' according to my CV.

Friday 30th May

I took the kids to see the flat this evening.

'It's a bit small, dad,' was Sean's reaction. Get used to it, son. Neither of the boys were exactly jumping up and down with excitement but they do understand that I am working to a budget. They were content with the location so I think it's a go. It is hardly a detached house in Surrey but it will have to do for the next year or so at least.

I haven't quite signed the paperwork yet as I wanted to come home and work out my finances just to be sure I can afford it. Having done the maths for about the tenth time, I am still not sure. I might have to reassess the amount I am paying to my ex. Strictly speaking I am paying her slightly more than I am obliged to by the proper authorities. If I reduce my payments to her, it won't go down well. I have got a tricky balance to strike there because if I reduce it by too much, she won't be able to afford to keep the house. And then the kids will suffer. If it wasn't for that little nuance, I would have been paying her less from the start.

Our trip to the flat was followed by a trip to the curry house. I love a good curry and decided today that it is about time I started educating my kids on the intricacies of Indian restaurant menus. My ex wouldn't have covered this vital life skill as she doesn't possess it herself.

We went to my old haunt, the Motspur Park Tandoori. Had we been there a couple of hours later we would have been joined by groups of inebriated revellers as they left the Earl Beatty pub next door, but with the sun still being high in the sky when we arrived, ours and another family were the only two groups in the restaurant.

'Whoever can eat the hottest curry can have an ice-cream for dessert,' I challenged them.

Ever the competitor, Jack took me up on the challenge and ordered a madras. Sean decided he didn't want to play and went for a korma. I couldn't let my eldest beat me so I asked the grinning waiter for a vindaloo. The curries arrived. Sean didn't care that he wouldn't win the contest and concentrated on enjoying his curry. Jack endured his curry. He wasn't bothered about the prize either but he did want to get one over on me. My curry was the hottest thing I have ever tasted despite me telling the chef whilst on my way to the toilet to go easy on the chillies. I failed woefully.

Of course we all ended up having ice cream. We had a great night. On the way home Jack and Sean told me that when I was in the toilet they had asked the waiter to add extra spice to my vindaloo.

Sunday 1ˢᵗ June

So yesterday I saw my ex out socially for the first time since she became my ex. Obviously she wasn't out socially with me but we were out socially at the same place, the Morden Brook.

The lads had arranged to meet up to give Andy a bit of a send-off before he moves to Canada next week. We had all bought him little mementos of our time together, mostly stupid stuff like an encyclopaedia of British beers, a poster of Greg Rusedski with 'he's British now' scrawled all over it and a Bear Grylls book about surviving in the wild. We were intending on having a good night.

And then my ex walked in. It pains me to admit it but she looked pretty good, in a new outfit of pillar-box red jeans and a leather jacket. She looked like she had lost a few pounds too.

I watched her walk up to the bar with her group of revellers. She hadn't noticed me at this point. I recognised a few of her crowd. Sarah and Debbie and a couple more mother's-union types and their respective husbands. But there were a few I didn't recognise, including the man who put his hand on my wife's left buttock as he was ordering the drinks.

All of a sudden I had gone from thinking I was having

a good time with my mates to being completely conscious of my single status. I thought I was making progress in my life but there I was, single, in the pub with my single mates, about to go back to my parents' and sleep on a mattress on the floor. My ex, who still hadn't noticed me, was with her group of married friends, with her new man and probably about to go back to my marital home with him and make noises that only I have heard her make for the past fifteen years. Actually someone had heard her at our golfing week-end in Sussex and banged on the hotel wall, but we will ignore that for now.

Was I jealous? Yes. And some.

She was flagrantly taking advantage of me having the kids for the night. I had spent the day with the boys and the dog in Bournemouth and dropped them off with my mum on my way round to the pub. I was tempted to get on the phone to my parents and tell them to send the kids home.

The married group didn't notice us single guys for quite a while. We had got there early and had occupied our favourite table in the back of the pub. I was the only one of our group to notice them too as my mates were all engrossed in pointing out things Andy won't miss on his trip to Canada (David Cameron, Strictly Come Dancing, the Tory party, come to think of it all British politicians, and the Northern Line). For some reason I felt the need to laugh loudly at all our jokes, as if to show my ex that I was having a better time than her. I got a few odd looks from Dave, Ray and Andy before Dave eventually cottoned on to the reason for my antics.

'Your ex scrubs up nicely,' he rather unhelpfully observed.

Eventually they saw us too and my ex waved to me. I watched as she whispered something to her new lover and he smiled knowingly. Why hadn't the kids mentioned this wanker to me? I took some small consolation from the fact that he was rather plain-looking, with a belly that definitely put him into the clinically obese category and hair that had seen better days.

'It's your round Graham.' Oh god, so I had to go up to the bar. I composed myself, mentally armed myself with all the witty put-downs I could think of and flexed my muscles in case things turned nasty.

'Hello Graham, nice garb for the pub,' my ex observed, gesturing to my shorts and trainers, still sandy from the beach (I still can't get rid of the trainers). I hadn't had time to change since coming back from Bournemouth.

'Is that a large wine you've got? I obviously pay you too much maintenance,' I said in response. My inner self was screaming at me not to show weakness. Or maybe it was the lads sitting at our table watching the encounter. Or just the beer talking.

My ex put on her best condescending look and was about to respond when her knight in shining armour entered the fray on her behalf. 'You must be Graham. I'm Mark.' He held his orange juice out as if he wanted me to clink glasses.

'Nice comb-over mate. If you ever so much as say a word to my children I swear I'll ruin your life,' I said, clashing my virtually empty pint glass into his high-class, up-your-own-pretentious-backside J2O with enough force to spill half his drink on his expensive-looking brogues.

'Oh grow up, Graham,' my ex said. I actually stuck my tongue out at them as they turned and re-joined their group of happy couples. I then stood feeling like Billy no mates at the bar waiting to be served for what seemed like an eternity.

Now, with the benefit of a night's sleep between me and last night's encounter, I can see that my antics weren't particularly sensible or mature. In an effort to show strength I showed weakness. My ex will get the impression that what she does still matters to me. She will take some satisfaction from sorting her life out quicker than me.

She will probably think I still care about her. Honestly, though, she would be wrong. I care about being part of a couple. I care about having someone to share things with. I care about having someone to sleep with. Seeing my ex last night just brought it all home to me. It isn't that I want to be back with my ex. I don't. I just want to be with someone. Yes, I am jealous that she has got there before me, but I didn't for one minute last night wish that I was mister comb-over. OK, maybe for one minute…

I learned a valuable lesson last night. Not the lesson you might be thinking of, but a completely different one. Always empty the sand from your trainers before you walk into the house. I spent half of my morning hoovering up the mess. I tried to blame the children but my parents, not to mention the boys, weren't having it.

Neither Jack nor Sean had any inkling as to who comb-over Mark was or where my ex met him. Without putting any pressure on them I asked them to let me know if they saw him about the house in the coming days. As far as I could tell he wasn't there when I dropped the boys off at their mum's after their respective cricket matches. My ex was though, standing hands on hips in the doorway. I apologised for my performance in the pub. 'Fuck off,' was her somewhat terse response. At least we are still on speaking terms.

I spent the afternoon diligently filling in a couple of application forms. I am not quite sure what an 'asset protection manager' is but I am sure I can Google it if they decide to interview me.

Tuesday 3rd June

I am now committed to renting the flat off Martin Way. I have paid far too much money over to the estate agents. Subject to references, I hope to be able to move in in a couple of weeks. I am still not sure I am doing the right thing but for my own self-esteem as much as anything, I need to have 'my own place'. I won't dwell yet on the fact that it isn't actually mine. I told my parents the good news.

My mum had one last ditch attempt to get me to go home to my ex. 'Graham, are you sure you can't just move back in to your old house? I am absolutely certain your family would still take you back if you asked.'

I thought about telling her about Mr comb-over but I didn't have the energy. Instead I just shrugged and told her it wasn't happening.

'Well if you won't go back then at least reassure us that you will continue bringing Jack and Sean round to see us,' she followed up. At what point do your parents start to care more about their daughter-in-law and their grandchildren than they do about their own children?

Amy and Susie the shih poo were waiting for us at the Windmill when Albus and I arrived tonight. To lay my cards on the table, I have really got the hots for Amy and it isn't just because it's been a while since, you know.

We had another great night dog-walking and drinking, at the end of which we at last exchanged phone numbers. Amy suggested that we should engineer a weekend dog walking 'chance' encounter when we had our kids with us.

I am not sure of the etiquette of dating when you have kids. At what point should you introduce your children to your date? I let my kids have a say in where I was thinking of living but there is no way I am letting them have a say in who I date. What if my kids don't get on with Amy or Lucy? What if Albus falls out with Susie? Lots of questions, but at the moment I am quite excited about the prospect of seeing Amy again. I don't want to compartmentalise my life too much, so let's chuck everything in the pot and see what happens.

Wednesday 4th June

The boys are off on a scouts' trip at the weekend so they came to see me this evening. My ex phoned me before dropping them off and gave me strict instructions that neither of them is allowed to play on any gaming devices. When I asked her why, she told me to ask them.

It isn't easy being a parent at the best of times, i.e. when you are living under one roof. My ex and I had one golden rule when we were parents and that was always agree with the other parent, however wrong they may be. I always tried my best to adhere to that one simple rule, which was why we came home from our camping trip to Devon after only one day all because my kids woke up early and my ex had a go at them.

I was a bit sceptical today though. Is it right for the ex to be punishing the kids when they are in my care? Maybe it is but if a punishment I dished out spanned in to her time with the boys, I have absolutely no faith that my ex would enforce it. She didn't always stick to her side of the bargain when we lived together. I would often come home from work to find the kids watching the telly despite me having banned them from watching it for a week for some misdemeanour or other. She would justify it by saying something inane like 'I needed to cook dinner' or 'leave them alone, they're tired'. Basically there was one rule for me and another for my ex.

When the boys arrived I asked them what they had done wrong to get them a gaming device ban. I had decided that if the punishment truly did fit the crime then I would still continue to support my ex. I might not be married to her anymore but we are still partners in the rearing of our children.

'Dad, it's not fair,' Sean complained, 'all we were doing was playing games on mum's phone.'

'She totally lost it with us and sent us to bed. I mean it's ridiculous dad, how old are we?' Jack joined in.

'She sent you to bed and banned you from computers for playing on her phone?' I asked. This didn't sound particularly feasible to me. The boys have spent half their childhoods playing with our phones.

'We might have read a facebook message that popped up when we were playing,' Jack conceded.

At this point I know I should have let it lie, or maybe even reinforced the importance of personal privacy. Instead I found myself asking about the message. My boys took great pleasure in telling me it was from Mark, aka Mr combover. He apparently messaged my ex thanking her for a great night and asking her over for dinner.

'That's not all it said though,' Sean threw in. As if that wasn't enough. 'This Mark guy went on to ask mum whether it was definitely over between you and her because he thought you were still in love with mum.' Excuse my language but who does the fucking idiot think he is?

'But don't worry dad, we put him straight,' Jack let on. Somewhat sheepishly I asked my son how he put my ex's new lover straight.

'We sent him a reply saying that mum has never been so

bored in her life, she thinks he's an idiot and never wants to see him again,' Jack explained.

'And don't forget the bit about him having a small penis,' my twelve-year-old chirped.

The boys and I had a great evening playing on the PS4.

Thursday 5th June

Do I or don't I phone Amy? It has only been two days since I saw her last. We agreed we would go out walking at some point with our respective children. Mine aren't with me this weekend. Does that mean I can't see Amy? Would it look odd if I phoned and suggested another adults-only dog walk? I am not officially going out with Amy so I don't want her to think I am being too pushy or too desperate. I mentioned my dilemma to Dave, who knows about these things.

'When your mum's dying of cancer you realise that life is too short to piss about,' he told me.

So I stopped being a wet fart and phoned her. Someone else, presumably her daughter Lucy, answered the call. I quickly went back to being a wet fart and hung up. My relationship with Amy seems destined either to be a slow burner or maybe even a spark that doesn't catch. I will try her again tomorrow.

Saturday 7th June

With the kids now ensconced in a tent somewhere in the rain, I have been left to my own devices for the weekend. Most of my own devices are now the property of my ex, so what that means in reality is that I have been surfing the net to find more jobs I can do. I said I wanted to work with animals but I draw the line at being a chicken sexer or a dog food tester – these can't be real jobs surely? I applied to be 'head of category management' for a stationery company. I have less of a clue about that one than I had about the asset protection manager job.

I have also been phoning Amy. Two, five, ten times in the last day or two. No one has answered my calls. Maybe she's avoiding me. I went over our last meeting in my head. I don't think I embarrassed myself. In fact, I thought I did pretty well and am pretty sure she had thought so too. But why isn't she returning my calls? I am not used to having Amy in my life but somehow I am already missing her. In the end I sent her a text. 'Fancy meeting me for dinner on Tuesday instead of walking the dog? Graham Hope.' She hasn't replied yet.

I don't know what possessed me to do it but I also checked out my ex's recent posts on Facebook. I got a shock. It's her birthday. I hadn't even realised. Although we didn't tend to make a big thing of our birthdays, I have never totally forgotten her birthday before.

I wonder how she is spending the day. The kids aren't with her because they are on camp. They hadn't mentioned her birthday to me but that doesn't surprise me. The boys only tend to remember their own birthdays. They wouldn't have brought her a present either because I hadn't given them any extra money to buy it with or kicked their backsides to go shopping.

The thought that it was my ex's birthday and I hadn't noticed actually depressed me a bit. It is just one more sign of how far apart we have drifted. How truly out of the non-kids part of her life I am. I am trying to see it as a positive: that it means I am getting over my ex, I am not attached to her like I used to be, I don't hang off her every word. The problem with that viewpoint, though, is that I keep checking her Facebook status all the time.

I bet my ex is struggling today, not being with her kids on her birthday. I sent her a Facebook message telling her I hope she has a good day and letting her know that the kids' present is on its way.

I could tell from the profile picture that one of the numerous birthday messages she had been sent on facebook was from Mr comb-over. 'Happy birthday sexy,' he had written for my ex and half the world to see. Whatever.

Sunday 8th June

Last night we had an impromptu final really final this time leaving party for Andy. We started off in the Prince of Wales in Wimbledon but for some reason ended up in a gay night club in Soho. It seems that wherever I go, I end up spending the evening propping up the bar with Andy while Dave lights up the dance floor and Ray struts around preening himself. Over our third or fourth Jagerbomb, Andy told me he thinks Ray is gay. I haven't known Ray for as long as I have known Dave and Andy and now that Andy mentions it I can't actually recall seeing Ray with a girl. My gaydar is pretty rubbish (anyone less obvious than Julian Clary would probably not show up) so for all I know Andy may have a point about Ray. It would certainly explain why we ended up at a gay night club.

The vibe in the club was good (my kids would LOL if they heard me using a phrase like that). Everyone got on with everyone. I am sure I was chatted up a couple of times. Why doesn't that happen when I go out to straight clubs? I texted my sister Hills and told her where I was.

'Gay bars are crap these days 'cos they are full of straight people like you,' was her reply.

That was last night. I have spent today recovering and catching up with my ex's activities on social media, a habit

I really must kick. Her latest Facebook update indicates that she wasn't sitting at home crying into her pillow on her birthday. She was 'punting' on the river Cam. And when I say punting I don't mean she was betting on it. And she was with Mr comb-over. She probably hadn't even noticed that the kids hadn't bought her a present. I won't bother buying her some tacky earrings on the boys' behalf then.

I received a long-awaited text from Amy too. Strangely, it read, 'I wasn't expecting that question via text!' God, what had I done? I thought I had texted Amy asking her if she fancied meeting up for dinner. What could have been wrong with that? I checked back and it turns out I had managed to press send prematurely. I had actually asked 'do you fancy me'. God what a muppet I am. She must have thought I'm some sort of weirdo. Who in their right mind would ask someone via text if they fancied them?

I spent some time thinking about how I could rectify the situation. I could text her explaining my mistake but knowing me I would probably cock that up too. In the end I just phoned her and told her of my error. After an awkward start to the conversation, Amy and I ended up laughing about my uselessness. She actually can't do Tuesday but we have agreed to meet up on Saturday with our respective children. I am still not sure if involving our offspring in our relationship at this early stage is the right thing to do but after my texting error I am just grateful she wants to meet up at all. Roll on Saturday.

Monday 9th June

Jack called in this evening on his way back from a school cricket match. He was full of the joys of spring. His school team had won. He had also had a good weekend at the scout camp. When I asked him whether he had missed anything noteworthy when he was away, he thought for a minute and said no.

'What about your mum's birthday?' I prompted.

'We might not have been there, but we gave her a present before we went.' It turns out that they had bought her a bottle of perfume, paid for through saving their pocket money for the last month.

'Why didn't you mention it to me?' I asked. 'I could have helped you out with the cost of the present.'

'Because you aren't married to mum anymore. She isn't your wife and you don't really like each other so why would you buy her a present?' Jack responded.

My boys are full of surprises. They have had to shoulder more responsibility because of their parents' divorce. I wish they hadn't had to but they seem to be doing us proud. I hate the way the divorce segregates our lives. Despite having a pretty good relationship with the boys, I don't get to share a lot of what they do. They are growing up fast and I am missing out on sharing big chunks of the process with them.

I sent Jack home with some cash for him and his brother towards the cost of buying their mum's present.

Once he had gone, I spent the rest of the evening looking up what an asset protection manager is as I received an email inviting me for an interview on Friday.

Wednesday 11th June

What do divorced parents do when it comes to school parents' evenings? Well, bearing in mind it was mine and my ex's first parents' evening as non-cohabiting parents, we decided we would both go. We took this decision partly because it is 'the right thing to do' but I suspect the real reason was that we didn't trust each other to report back.

The evening went quite well. We managed not to dwell for too long on Mr comb-over. I did discover my ex had given the kids some money a couple of weeks ago towards the cost of her present. I shall be having words with my eldest boy, the cheeky git.

Our first appointment of the evening was with Sean's form teacher. I didn't drool too publicly over her and in return she didn't mention that she had seen my naked arse in Morden swimming baths. Then it was on to Sean's English teacher. She was positively gushing in her praise for his creative writing and particularly liked his imaginative piece on the impact of a parental split on two brothers.

His RE, music and art teachers told us off for not bothering to make an appointment to see them. My response that Sean is never going to be a vicar, a famous composer or an impressionist painter, so what was the point in seeing them?

In response his art teacher pointed out that he had seen Sean playing football and in his opinion Sean is never going to be a famous footballer so we needn't bother going to see the PE teacher either. A bit rude but probably fair enough.

A couple of Jack's teachers did comment on his work going downhill as the year progressed, which was slightly concerning.

My kids (sorry, our kids) are pretty bright and keen to learn. I have a basic rule that I try to instil in Jack and Sean. Whatever they do, they should be proud of themselves. This rule is easy to say but harder to live your life by. When I was at school, I would often rush work so that I could get out and play football. My kids are just the same. They won't always prioritise their homework. But I suspect they've been even less likely to prioritise it over the last few months as neither of their parents has been nagging them as much as we used to. When I only see the kids for a day here and a day there, I confess I don't spend the whole time making sure they are proud of their work. I feel a bit guilty about this but I am also learning that sometimes in life you have to adapt your approach as a parent. For the past few months, being there for my boys has seemed more important than the daily grind of completing online maths questions, writing about some artist no one has ever heard of or discussing which invention was the most influential in facilitating the industrial revolution.

In a rare moment of harmony between us, my ex and I agreed on the way out of the parents' evening that we would focus more on supporting our children at school. We will make more effort to build homework into our parenting timetable (not that we actually have a parenting timetable) and we will help Jack and Sean to make sure they have the right books in the right place at the right time to do their school work. Jack's incident with his geography books a couple of months ago wasn't an isolated incident. The kids need to take responsibility for their own work, but as parents we haven't made it easy for them. If my ex and I were given a school report for being parents, the teacher would have written 'could do better'.

Friday 13th June

The kids stayed over with me last night. They wanted to watch the first World Cup game with me.

The World Cup is an excuse for quality father and son time. The ex knows absolutely nothing about football and used to repeatedly embarrass herself at little league by cheering the opposition's goals. So the kids jumped at the chance of watching the opening game with me. It didn't start until late so the opportunity to stay up late on a school night probably also had an impact on their considerations.

I am not a complete football anorak but I do love the World Cup. I have been known to hang a flag out of my bedroom window for at least the five minutes that England are still in the tournament. Obviously I would tell the neighbours that the kids twisted my arm to do it but really I am the one that enjoys showing his patriotism.

Brazil beat Croatia thanks, in part, to a Japanese referee.

Both boys went to school this morning looking absolutely knackered. So much for my good intentions after the parents' evening.

I was knackered too. Watching the football and having a few cans of London Pride wasn't the ideal preparation for my job interview.

After queueing for the shower and washing the sleep out

of my eyes, I dusted off my best suit (literally), picked out my most conservative-looking tie and took the tube to Old Street to go and talk about protecting assets. This was my first job interview for a few years. I don't mind interviews but I usually prefer the ones in which I know a bit about the subject in hand. My basic Google searches didn't exactly qualify me as an expert in preventing fraud, in buying CCTV systems and training staff in asset protection but I reckon I managed to talk the talk at least to the extent that I didn't look like a complete twat. The one question I struggled with was when they asked me what experience I had in conducting interrogations to identify staff engaged in criminal activity. I resisted the urge to talk about my degree in waterboarding, my fanaticism with Spooks on the BBC and my apprentice-ship at Guantanamo Bay. In the end I opted to talk about my problem-solving abilities.

Apparently they will let me know whether I got the job or not next week. I won't be waiting with bated breath for their call.

I went straight to work after my interview. The most productive thing I did all afternoon was organise the office World Cup sweepstake. I got a few dirty looks from Daniel boss-man who thought I should have been spending my time pouring over some vital spreadsheet or other. Still, it was worth the dirty looks. I got Argentina so at least I am in with a chance of winning a few quid.

Saturday 14th June

Today's big event was the walk on Wimbledon Common with Jack and Sean. How can walking the dog be 'a big event'? Well, in my book it can if it involves an 'accidental' meeting with Amy, her daughter Lucy and Susie the shih poo. Jack and Sean are normally quite happy to take the dog for a walk, so long as they get at least one cake at some point on the walk. Today for some reason they weren't too bothered about going out but once I upped the ante to the promise of a take-away pizza when we got home, they agreed to come.

The nerves had kicked in big time before this meeting. Would I show myself up in front of Amy and her daughter? Would my kids show me up? Would the presence of the kids hamper mine and Amy's efforts to get to know each other? Would the whole thing go tits up? I was particularly nervous about meeting Amy's daughter. My experience of interacting with teenage girls was practically zero. Even including when I was a teenager myself. I haven't got a clue what you talk to teenage girls about. They generally don't do football, curries and arm wrestles. What if Lucy turned out to be a brat?

I had a shave this morning and then put on my best chinos and the shoes that the boys had made me buy. I even dug out a bottle of aftershave that my ex had bought me ages ago and splashed it on in all the right places. I even groomed the bloody dog.

'Dad, you stink,' Sean told me in the car on the way to the Common. Thanks son. I had thought about nagging the boys to dress up too but I couldn't work out how I would justify it so in the end I left them to choose their own clothes – an Angry Birds top for Sean and an already dirty rugby shirt for Jack. Not exactly designer clothing but it could have been worse, I suppose.

As luck and a few surreptitious text messages would have it, just as we arrived at the Windmill Amy was strolling across the car park with her entourage. Lucy was a pint-sized version of her mum. They both wore cut-off jeans. Lucy had a sparkly crop top on (I could have sworn I caught Jack checking her out) and her mother wore a cosy-fitting black top (Jack almost certainly caught me checking her out).

Much raucous barking ensued as Albus and Susie reacquainted themselves with each other. Tails were wagged, audible greetings exchanged and backsides sniffed. I wish I could adopt the dogs' uncomplicated approach and carefree attitude although I would have drawn the line at the sniffing backsides bit.

Amy and I at least had an excuse this time for not being overly familiar with each other. We had a pretence to keep up. We exchanged the normal pleasantries that you would expect your average anonymous dog walkers to share, we confirmed that we were going in the same direction and began our stroll.

At one point when it became clear that we wouldn't be going off in different directions at the next fork in the path, Lucy took her headphones off and introductions were made. Jack and Lucy seemed to be chatting or at least what passes for chatting in a teenage context. Sean was content to throw sticks for the dogs.

The only downside on the walk came when Albus chased Susie into the most stagnant, repugnant pond on the common. No walk would be complete without Albus getting himself filthy. I have got a clapped out old people carrier that was stained from previous dog walks so I had no problem with my dog's antics. Amy felt slightly differently and tried to drag Susie out of the pond before the little dog was completely covered in gunk.

'Mum's worried about the state of her Porsche,' I heard Lucy telling Jack and Sean.

God, she must be loaded. Anyway, Amy's attempt to rescue her dog was doomed to fail as Susie emerged from the weed-infested lake looking like the dog version of the incredible hulk. The kids saw the funny side, even if Amy took a bit more convincing.

The afternoon stroll ended in a meal at the Hand in Hand. The kids readily agreed to forego their promised pizza so long as I let them have the most chocolate-laden dessert on the menu. The day was a great success, although I was left wondering again about the wisdom of bringing your kids to meet a prospective date before anything romantic had actually developed. Still, Amy and I are going to go out for a drink one night next week without dogs or children so that must be some sort of indication that the afternoon was good for her too.

Jack is more perceptive than I give him credit for. On the way home, he asked me whether I was going to see Amy again.

'Why do you want to know?' I replied.

'Because if you are, you need to get a haircut and lose the shapeless T-shirts.'

Thanks son, you sound so much like your mother.

The day ended badly. The boys and I watched England lose to Italy in the football.

Monday 16th June

So, today I found out that my detailed critique of my work's strategic review proposals had no impact whatsoever. They have confirmed their original proposals for a 'restructuring of our operations and a consequent repositioning of our staffing resources' which, for me, means that I have to compete for a job with short skirt Sarah, the brown-nosing attractive little miss perfect. They are hoping to get all of the restructuring done by the time people go off for their summer holidays. How considerate of them.

I also got the predictable news that I didn't get that asset protection manager job. On reflection I think I was a bit naïve even going for it. I need a new job but I probably should be focussing my efforts on vacancies that I at least have some chance of being offered. I did read in the paper the other day that they are recruiting for staff to work in the passport offices. Maybe I should apply for one of those vacancies. Sean's passport still hasn't come through. I could process his application.

It is a bit early to start panicking but I am beginning to fear that my decision to move into a rented flat might have been slightly rash. But shit happens to those that let shit happen to them, so I must keep looking for new jobs and not be thrown off-course at the first adverse wind.

Talking of the flat, I started thinking about packing today. Friday is moving in day. Having lost most of my stuff to my ex, I actually don't have much to move so I ended up only thinking about packing. Five minutes on Thursday night should do the trick.

Tuesday 17th June

I may have shot myself in the foot again today. This afternoon I was supposed to be filling in a work performance evaluation report on our lorry fleet, but instead I thought I would spend some time discreetly filling in a 'programme office manager' job application. Unfortunately, when I went to make a cup of tea, Daniel came over to see my workstation and spotted the application on my screen. He sent me the following email:

> *'Graham, I happened to pass your monitor just now. We pay you to work, not to search for new jobs on our time. I respectfully suggest that you pull your finger out and complete the logistics performance report before you go home tonight.*
>
> *By the way, I found your job application an interesting read, particularly the bit where you claimed credit for 'single-handedly transforming the company's operating processes to achieve efficiencies worth more than £1 million per year.' If I was you, I would suggest that you add 'excellent imagination' to the exhaustive list of skills you claim, on page two of your application, to possess.'*

Arsehole.

OK, so maybe I was being a bit economical with the truth in my application, but who isn't? Note to self, don't ask Danny boy to write me a reference.

Thursday 19th June

Tonight is my last night living with my parents. Looking back on the last few months, there were some initial teething troubles but we soon got into a routine and coexisted without too many issues. I am grateful to my parents for giving me a place to stay for a few months. Their house was just about big enough for the kids to stay at from time to time although the queues for the bathroom won't be missed. Neither will the attempts to get me to go back to my ex.

Without wishing to be ungrateful to my parents for what they have done, I can't wait to become an independent, fully functioning adult again. I am not sure how often I will use it, but I want the freedom to walk naked around the flat when I want to, to invite my mates round for a few beers (not while I am naked obviously), to eat in front of the telly, to sit on the loo with the toilet door open if there is something good I am listening to on the radio and even to leave the hoovering until tomorrow if that's what I decide to do. I need my own place.

The boys came over tonight, partly to show solidarity in thanking their grandparents for their hospitality but mostly to watch the England match. Another World Cup over before it has even begun for England.

Friday 20th June

I am writing today's update from my new abode. I can tick that goal off then. The flat has two bedrooms. The master bedroom has a double bed, a pine wardrobe with doors that don't shut properly and a scratched up table and chair with a view out of the window overlooking the road and the number 164 bus stop. The walls are off-white, as they are throughout the flat.

You can tell that a previous set of occupants used the second bedroom as a children's bedroom. There are two single beds in there already, the pine frames of which are adorned with the remnants of stickers that someone has made a token effort to try and remove. The wallpaper around the beds is beginning to peel off, probably as a result of bored little fingers fiddling with it after lights out. A quirky comic strip light shade – the only lightshade in the whole flat – has also managed to outlast the previous tenants.

As well as the bedrooms, I have a decent sized albeit completely dull and characterless sitting room, equipped with a sofa and an armchair as well as a basic dining table and chairs. There is a dark wood TV table in the corner that is too small to accommodate my large telly, so I have had to mount the telly on the dining table for now.

The best thing that can be said for the kitchen and bathroom is that everything seems to work. I am not sure I will be able to fully relax in the bath until I have disinfected it several times. The cooker is filthy too. Looking on the bright side, at least I won't have to clean the flat to high standards when I move out.

The move went as well as could be expected. When my ex and I moved to our (now her) detached pad in Surrey, we had two lorries full of stuff. Now, I can comfortably fit my worldly possessions into the back of my car.

If truth be told I am feeling a bit crap tonight. I can't help thinking about how far I have fallen. My ex is still in our detached house, the most expensive house in the street. I am in a flat on a main road in Morden.

I am trying not to dwell on my previous life but I can't help recalling summers spent in the garden with our huge paddling pool and table tennis table. The neighbours' kids used to drop in just to play in our garden. There will be none of that here.

Like missing my ex's birthday, this move feels like I am hammering another nail into the coffin that contains our relationship. I won't share time with my ex in this flat. She will have no association with it. I thought I had already got my head around mine and my ex's separation, but tonight I am really coming to realise the permanence of it all.

Even moving from my parents' to here is hard. I have hardly spent any time on my own at my parents'. I am now in a flat where for most of the time Albus and I will be the only occupants. That is going to take some getting used to.

I am still convinced that in the long run moving out of my parents' is the right thing to do. Living with my mum and dad always felt temporary. I couldn't entertain there, I couldn't make my mark on the property or give it my personality. I couldn't bring women back. So moving into my own place, however shitty it is, has to be the right thing to do. Maybe I need to feel lonely to give me the push to get off my backside and sort my life out.

Now that I have moved away from my parents I can do whatever I want. The trouble is, I am now asking myself what 'whatever I want' looks like in reality. I haven't exactly got a queue of women waiting to come over for wild parties. I am not even sure that I would want to bring Amy here (I am being presumptuous even thinking that she might want to come). What would she make of this flat? She drives a Porsche and lives off the Ridgway for god's sake. Would she approve of the England flag hanging out of the window?

Because I haven't lived on my own since god knows when, and because my parents have done the cooking for the last few months, I need to reacquaint myself with a frying pan. My mum bought me a cook book as a house-moving present. She is fretting that I will live off takeaways and ready meals. She may well be right to fret. It isn't that I can't cook but I am not sure how inclined I will be to go to the effort of cooking when I am only cooking for one.

I flicked through the cook book. I am a bit of a snob when it comes to food. I am partial to take-away curries but generally want proper fresh English meat and vegetables. Having said that, I pushed the boat out tonight and cooked a big spag bol – the Italian type that takes hours to cook rather than the British type where you chuck everything in a pan with a jar of sauce. So there!

Spag bol, a bottle of lager or six and watching the World Cup. It shouldn't have been a bad night. But I couldn't get excited by Honduras versus Ecuador. More significantly I can't seem to shake off the loneliness. And the flat was so quiet when the football had finished and the telly was off.

I am not used to quiet, so I put the radio in the kitchen on before I went to bed to create the illusion that I am not alone.

The kids are coming round tomorrow and then I have dinner with Amy so tomorrow shouldn't be as bad as tonight.

Saturday 21st June

And there was me worrying about how quiet it would be. At about midnight I discovered that my neighbour is also an 80s rock fan. I like Def Leppard as much as the next middle aged soft rock enthusiast, but I could have done without hearing 'Pour Some Sugar On Me' ten times over in the middle of the night. I think he was head-banging too. Personally I never got the point of head-banging. I never got the long hair and studs thing either.

Jack was playing cricket so only Sean came round in the end this afternoon. We did some web surfing to personalise the flat a bit. I hope Jack likes the Chelsea duvet cover. We put a few photos up in their bedroom to make it look more homely and relevant to their lives, and then Sean ate some of my spag bol before going off to a sleepover with some mates. I resisted the spag bol because I am going out on the town tonight with Amy.

It has been a while.

Sunday 22nd June

OK, so I need to tell you how last night went. Well, I should say up front, just to manage your expectations, that it has still been a while.

Amy and I went to the Spotted Horse in Putney, a fairly unadventurous, traditional pub with a decent atmosphere, particularly in the winter months by virtue of the fact that it has an open fire. The choice of pub was Amy's and her decision was influenced by the fact that Lucy was ill and was staying at her dad's in Earlsfield, so Amy wanted to be somewhere fairly close in case she had to jump in a cab and pick her up in a hurry. I did wonder if my ex followed similar logic and went out on dates to pubs in Morden when I last had the kids when they were ill. I doubt it somehow. I also vaguely wondered whether Amy was half hoping that her ex would see her out on a date. I probably shouldn't assume that Amy is as devious as me.

Amy looked stunning tonight, dressed in a simple but elegant black number. I wish I could describe it better but I am a bloke after all. Her hair is beautiful and striking, her skin pale but blemish-free and her smile just makes me melt. For the football lovers out there, Amy is undoubtedly Premier League. She might be Spurs or Everton rather than the

144

real top dogs of Manchester City or Chelsea, but she's certainly right up there. I am probably your Nottingham Forest – had the odd glory day but now a bit tired and dated. If Amy had been your supermodel, your Man City or Chelsea, she wouldn't have so much as looked at me. As it is, if Amy and I come to anything then I am definitely punching above my weight.

I bought the first round of drinks. This didn't seem like a lager night to me so I went with Amy's suggestion of getting a bottle of wine to share. Being no wine expert, I let Amy choose and we ended up with a cool Australian chardonnay. Over our first glasses we each gave the other a brief life history. (Mine: 'University, marriage, two kids, divorce, new flat'; hers: 'Grew up in Wimbledon, marriage to rich financier, one kid, hubby had affair with au pair, divorce, dog.') We then moved on to jobs. I told her about single-handedly bringing about efficiency savings of £1 million per year and she told me she lives off the proceeds of her divorce but also makes a few quid writing for a website for bored housewives.

But the most interesting conversation was about our children. Not general background stuff on what they are like, but very specific stuff. It turns out that Jack and Lucy have been texting each other non-stop for the past week and Lucy is trying hard to resist telling Jack that she has a crush on him. I haven't seen Jack all week so I hadn't picked up on this surprising development. I say surprising because despite Jack talking a bit more about girls over the last year or so, going to an all-boys school, as far as I know he has never actually progressed this interest into anything so much as a conversation with a girl. He still prefers to spend all his waking hours playing sports.

Anyway, with the wine consumed, the evening ended on a very pleasant note. We did exchange a kiss, and on the lips too, not some perfunctory peck on the cheek. This momentous coming together happened as the cab we were sharing stopped outside iron gates that presumably hid Amy's home behind them. I was half-hoping, no I was completely hoping, that she would ask me in for coffee but she didn't. Instead, she told me how much she had enjoyed the night and hoped we would do it again soon. There was a bit of an awkward pause and then Amy opened the cab door. She was climbing out before I decided I had to kiss her. I don't know where my confidence to make the first physical move came from but I rushed out of the cab after her, grabbed her hand and turned her towards me. The kiss itself was probably a bit of a lunge, a bit of a clash of my lips upon hers with a bit of nose bumping going on too but once Amy had realised that she wasn't being mugged, there was definitely two people participating in the kiss. Well, three if you count the cab driver who was standing next to us making sure we weren't about to do a runner.

I slept in late this morning, because I can. I am pretty chuffed with how last night went. Can I now officially say I am in a relationship? Maybe I can but who would I tell? Not my single mates as they will just take the piss. I could tell my ex but I would only be doing that to make myself feel good. She wouldn't be interested. I could have told the boys when they came round for tea tonight but I decided that it is too early to get into it with them. Having said that, when Jack got in the front door, he had a smug grin on his face. With a knowing expression, he asked what I got up to last night. I took it on the chin and resisted the temptation to tell him that I know his secret as well as him knowing mine. He will tell me about what is going on with him and Lucy when he is good and ready.

The boys and I had spag bol converted into a chilli for tea

(I think I might freeze the rest now). After living in the flat for the weekend, personalising it and having the kids round, I feel much happier about the move. We will do our best to make some good memories here.

Monday 23ʳᵈ June

For some reason this morning, all of my radios were tuned to Capital. I tried other presets and they had been changed too, to things like XFM, 6music and Radio 1. I might occasionally cope with Capital, but I am more a Radio 2 and Magic man these days. Still, at least the kids felt at home enough to mess with my stuff.

I got a date for my interview for my current job today. Basically, I will be put out of my misery on Friday. In the circumstances, sloping off from work early to watch the Holland versus Chile game on the telly probably wasn't my wisest decision of the year but I went anyway.

Tuesday 24th June

Phew, Sean's passport arrived. I had to go and pick it up from my ex's today. I used her address as I suspect it was the one they had on the database and I didn't want to complicate things.

When I went round there, my ex told me Sean was out with his mates and Jack was out with his girlfriend. I am sure my ex was hoping to surprise me with that news because she couldn't hide her look of disappointment when I just nodded. I asked my ex what she knew about his girlfriend. She said absolutely nothing, other than that he was always texting her. I felt slightly pleased that I knew something that she didn't.

My ex and I managed to stay on civil terms with each other this time. My evening with Amy is still fresh on my mind and has had the effect of reducing my bitterness that my ex is seeing someone. We even remained civil when I mentioned the thorny issue of maintenance payments again. I told her I had entered my income into an online maintenance calculator and its conclusion was that I was paying nearly twice as much as I needed to. I also told her about potentially (or should I say probably) losing my job. She took this news quite well and told me to pay whatever I could afford. She must definitely be loved up.

I spent longer in my old house this evening than I have spent there since my divorce came through. Whenever I go there these days I feel awkward. Part of me wants to go through the house with a fine tooth comb to see what I might have left behind and what has happened to the place since I have gone. Strangely my ex still has our wedding photo on her sitting room wall. The landscape prints from places we have visited are all still up, as is the framed picture of the two of us with the Grand Canyon as a backdrop. My former life confronts me wherever I look in my ex's home. I asked my ex why she hadn't had a revamp of the pictures tonight. 'Because the boys like to have your photo up,' she replied. That's funny, they haven't asked me to put any photos of their mum up in my new flat.

I also noticed my Bose stereo speaker sitting gathering dust on a shelf under the coffee table. I haven't got a decent sound system in my flat so when my ex was making us a cup of tea in the kitchen I quickly snuck the speaker out to my car.

Thursday 26th June

I've been in bed for a couple of days with a horrible sick bug. I won't go in to details. The timing is bad as I am due to have my interview for my job tomorrow. Daniel boss man isn't inclined to view me in a good light at the best of times so I am sure he thinks I am pulling a couple of sickies to watch the World Cup and prepare for my interview. Admittedly I have been doing the former. Tomorrow, when he hears my answers, any thoughts he had about me doing the latter will be well and truly dispelled.

Friday 27th June

I still don't feel great but I dragged myself in to work today, looking maybe not quite resplendent but certainly better than normal on a Friday in my 'interview suit and tie'.

It is hard applying for the job you currently do. You can't exaggerate your skills or achievements as the interviewers know you. It is harder still applying for your own job when your boss, who is conducting the interview, thinks you are an arse. And to top it all off, it is even harder still to apply for your own job when the competition turns up in a short skirt, a figure-hugging top showing a slightly inappropriate amount of cleavage and rather suspiciously walks in to the office at the same time as the boss.

Before I let off steam about the interview, I just want to register the fact that I am actually bloody good at my job. I am not the bumbling fool that I might sometimes make myself sound, at least not where my job is concerned anyway. I do what needs doing and sometimes go the extra mile when I think it will be appreciated. Daniel, my less-than-generous boss, conceded in my last appraisal that I was 'a valued member of the team'. Mind you I am sure he plays bullshit bingo when it comes to appraisals.

So, to the interview. As well as Daniel, Michelle, the head of HR, was also sitting across the table from me. I have met

Michelle a few times, mostly in the pub after work. Considering she is an HR person, I actually quite like her.

Daniel kicked off the interview by asking me what my greatest achievement was in my current role. I swear he was grinning as he asked it. I steered clear of the million pound efficiencies line and talked instead about introducing monitoring systems that resulted in a reduction in the down-time of our vehicle fleet and a consequential improvement to our distribution network. Daniel pushed back, saying that there must be something I am even more proud of.

'Like what?' I asked.

'Like single-handedly transforming the company's operating processes to achieve efficiencies worth more than £1 million per year,' he replied.

'It's kind of you to mention that feat,' I told him. I admitted to being proud of my work to achieve efficiencies, but told him that anyone who claimed they single-handedly brought about efficiencies wouldn't be a team player, doesn't know the meaning of the word partnership, is selfish and short-sighted and in it for themselves. Not the sort of person who should be working for this company, I told him. I just about managed to keep a straight face as I ticked off a whole host of good-sounding nonsense.

I reckon I got the upper hand on that question. I let my advantage slip on the next one though. Michelle asked me what one thing I would change in the organisation to bring about improvement. 'My boss,' I replied. When I pick up my P45 in the near future, I will at least take some satisfaction from the fact that I made the head of HR laugh in my interview.

On a serious point, I am now even more worried than I was previously about my cash-flow. I will surely lose my job soon. I haven't got a clue how I will pay my rent in the long-term, or even the medium term, without a salary coming in.

Maybe I should try and be nice to my ex so she accepts a few 'I owe yous' in place of actual money for a couple of months. I really need to pull my finger out and get another job.

I haven't dwelt for too long on my performance at interview or my perilous financial situation because Jack and Sean have come to stay for a long weekend. Their mum has gone off to Exeter again to be with her ill dad. I am thankful for the fact that there hasn't been any recent talk of a permanent move to Exeter.

Saturday 28th June

After I wrote yesterday's update, the kids and I slobbed out in front of the telly, scoffed too much chocolate and watched a film, because for the first night in ages there wasn't any football on. I was thinking something Harry Potter-related but the kids are growing up. We watched Shaun of the Dead. I hated the film with a passion but it did remind me of a dispute between my ex and I when our own Sean was born. We agreed we would call our new baby Sean. Both of us liked the name. Sean was ill the day we were going to go and register his birth so I got the job of going to the registry office on my own. Sean Hope is actually registered as Shaun Hope because I didn't know you could spell the name any other way. When she saw the birth certificate my ex didn't speak to me for a week.

Jack and I have now come clean with each other about the women in our lives. He was texting away at the breakfast table. When I asked him who he was texting, he told me he would tell me if I told him who I went out with last Saturday night. Fair enough. I told him I met Amy and we had a nice evening and are planning to meet up again. He told me he had seen Lucy after school a couple of times. Their first get-together was for a hot chocolate and cookies in Centre Court shopping centre (her choice) and the second was a Burger King (my son the romantic's choice).

Once Sean had polished off his cornflakes and left the flat to go to the park with his mates, Jack put on a very worried look and asked me what he should do if Lucy wants to kiss him.

Now I don't know about other dads, but I have sometimes wondered if my son would ask me this sort of question. As I have previously pointed out, Jack is a real novice with the girls. Although we haven't talked about it too much, I think he feels awkward around them (I know how he feels). I know some of the other kids of his age have had numerous girlfriends already and their dads have either been asked for advice or have just given it whether they have been asked or not. But this is my first time having a proper grown up conversation with Jack about this stuff. I felt as nervous as Jack looked. Strangely though, I also felt really pleased to be asked. At least someone thinks I know what I am talking about when it comes to matters connected to the opposite sex.

So, how to respond to Jack's question of what he should do if Lucy wants to kiss him? A few answers ran through my mind, including:

a.   Go and ask your mother;

b.   Run a mile

c.   Run two miles

d.   Do you want to kiss her? If so, then give it a go. But make sure your mates aren't watching because if they see you kissing her they will take the piss forever.

After much deliberation I opted for a version of d) but without the mates bit. Jack was a bit embarrassed but did confess that, 'I don't mind a kiss like you and mum give me but I don't want to do any of that sloppy stuff where you each stick your tongue down each other's throats.'

'And what about hand-holding, is that acceptable in your book or not?' I asked.

'What's so good about holding hands? I've only just got mum to stop holding my hand when I cross Grand Drive,' Jack moaned.

'Don't worry son, you don't have to do anything you don't want to do,' I told him rather lamely.

'And she got a bit funny with me when I wouldn't meet her on Tuesday because I had cricket practice,' Jack was on a roll now.

'Welcome to life, son.' It suddenly dawned on me at this point how Jack is at a real crossroads in his development. One minute he's still a boy who will happily give his dad a kiss, but the next minute he is wrestling with decisions about how far to go with his girlfriend. I vowed there and then to buy him lots of ice-cream, take him to see Disney films and generally enjoy his childhood for as long as I possibly can.

At the end of our father and son chat, Jack still seemed to value my opinion which pleases me no end.

I resisted telling Jack that I was having similar dilemmas about what I should or shouldn't do with his girlfriend's mother.

Sunday 29th June

What is better than a stroll along the banks of the Thames with an attractive woman on a Sunday morning followed by a good lunch? Not a lot in my book. This morning, Jack and I between us made some phone calls and arranged to meet Amy and Lucy at Putney Bridge and walk along the river to Chiswick for a spot of lunch. Sean came with us, although I have a feeling that if mine and Amy's and Jack and Lucy's relationships develop, we may have to persuade Sean to continue coming on such walks with us.

Amy looks just as good in shorts and sandals as she does in jeans and boots. We kissed upon meeting today. That must go down as another step forwards. I didn't see any crafty kissing going on between Lucy and Jack but with the pair of them loitering at the back of our little group, I definitely spotted some awkward hand-holding.

We lunched at the City Barge pub by the river. With Amy and I getting to know each other, Jack and Lucy feeling each other out metaphorically speaking at least, Amy and I checking out our children's potential suitors and Sean beginning to get a sense of what was going on, lunch was interesting to say the least. At one point Amy asked Jack and Sean what they liked best about school.

'Nothing,' Sean offered.

And from Jack, 'The bell for going home.'

I wasn't having my kids down-playing their academic abilities so I told Amy and Lucy proudly that my boys were doing pretty well at school and were both in the 'gifted and talented' programme. Jack kicked me under the table and chastised me on the way home for making him out to be some sort of teacher's pet.

I sensed that Amy fell in to the same trap as me when she told Jack and Sean that she and Lucy used to enter gymkhanas and win rosettes on their own horses. Why do I always fall for people who like horses? I can't stand the animals, they give me asthma. Lucy told her mum to shut up because she was embarrassing her.

It was an odd lunch, where Amy and I were both trying to big up our children's achievements to make them look attractive to the other. At about the time our traditional rhubarb crumble and custard was delivered, Sean couldn't take listening to any more of my complimentary comments about Jack.

'Dad,' he protested, 'why don't you tell Lucy about the time Jack came home crying because Ivor Cox had beaten him up when he scored a goal past him in football practice. Or what about the time when he got in to trouble at school for refusing to go swimming because he didn't want to get his willy out in the changing room?' He just about finished his last sentence before chairs started falling over and he ended up on the floor.

'Thank god I haven't got a brother,' Lucy said to Jack as Sean re-took his seat at the table, still with a smile on his face.

On the walk back towards Putney Bridge, Amy and I found ourselves ahead of the children who had gone to retrieve the dogs from behind a boat house. We laughed about our awkward attempts to big up our respective children. Jack and Lucy were getting on like a house on fire without us needing to egg them on. I am not sure what I make of Jack seeing Lucy. Part of me can't help thinking 'good on you son'. But another part, the more mature part, worries that it is just too early for Jack to get into girls. Up until a couple of months ago he was quite happy playing his sport. I admired his simple life. He was happy when he was playing, ecstatic when he was playing well but miserable when his team lost. We all knew where we stood. But now that he has met Lucy, it is harder to work out what is going on in his head. When I mentioned this to Amy, her answer didn't exactly reassure me.

'I wouldn't read too much into Lucy and Jack's relationship. Lucy's boyfriends tend to come and go pretty quickly.'

The kids re-joined us at that point so I didn't get the chance to ask Amy whether the same could be said of her boyfriends.

Tuesday 1ˢᵗ July

I think I now know why my ex was being nice to me last week. Today when she was picking up the kids she dropped the bombshell that she was taking them off to Antigua for three weeks a few days after I get back from Turkey with them in August. Three weeks in Antigua. And in their own private villa too. Well, that has well and truly trumped my Turkey trip. I should be pleased for the kids that they will be getting a great holiday, but I must admit that my most prominent emotions when the ex told me about the holiday were envy and self-pity. Envy soon evolved into anger when I thought of how much a holiday like that would cost.

'I bet you are paying for that trip out of my maintenance payments, aren't you?' I asked.

'No, actually Mark's parents own the villa so we only have to pay for the flights,' she replied.

Mr comb-over. Not only is she whisking my kids off to Antigua for three weeks, but they are going with her new man.

I really and truly don't care that my ex has got a new bloke, but I can't get the thought out of my head that this new bloke is going to be spending longer with Jack and Sean this summer than I am. He will be making memories with my kids that I should be making.

I wanted to say something that would be a show-stopper. Something that would make her realise that she can't take Jack and Sean away for half the summer without me and with some strange bloke.

'Don't you need injections to go to Antigua?' I rather lamely asked.

'Mark says you don't need anything that they haven't had already, and in any case the kids aren't frightened of a nurse's needle like you are,' my ex took pleasure in telling me.

I need a beer. Fortunately so does Dave, so we are off to the Morden Brook to watch the football.

Wednesday 2nd July

Last night's drink turned into a real session. Dave and I found it impossible to refuse the Brook's World Cup special - four pints for a tenner. It turns out that we also had something to celebrate. I asked Dave about the birdie he picked up on the golf course the last time I saw him.

'Oh, that cow,' he replied, 'she's old news. I am back with Lou now.'

I nearly choked on my lager. By Lou he means Louise, his ex-wife. The one who ran off with the librarian about five years ago. Well that is a turn-up for the books, no pun intended. Dave went on to tell me that Lou wants her old rock and roll lifestyle back. I just hope the librarian gets fined for taking five years to return her.

'Any chance of you getting back with your ex?' Dave asked me after a few more drinks.

'There's more chance of England being given a wild card in to the World Cup final and winning it,' I assured him. They have already flown home.

Dave's situation is very different from mine. He hasn't quite admitted as much to us but Ray, Andy and I have often speculated that Dave has never stopped loving Louise. I don't hold such intense feelings for my ex. I certainly can't see myself wanting to have her back five years from now. If I do, then something will have gone wrong in my life.

I do envy Dave though. He has got a real spring in his step. If even a fraction of the stories he told last night about his reconciliation with Lou are true, I especially envy him the amount of sex he is getting. God, Amy and I need to move our relationship on to the next level. I long to feel the thrill of being intimate with a woman again. The awkwardness of the first time. The feeling of closeness afterwards. I long to hold Amy in my arms as we drift off to sleep.

Enough already.

As hangovers go, this morning's was bad. I stumbled out of bed and just about managed to make the bathroom despite the world spinning around me. Copious amounts of coffee, Coke (the drink), water and any pills I could get my hands on didn't seem to help.

I eventually managed to muster up enough co-ordination to do my shirt buttons up and struggle into work. I now wish I hadn't bothered. Short skirt Sarah was shrieking and dancing in the corridors as I got to my desk. Oh, my head. Sarah's antics could only mean one thing. Daniel took great delight in telling me that I didn't get my job. It took all my effort not to throw up on the desk as he was giving me the news.

My boss did say that there were a couple of junior admin jobs in the organisation that I could do if I was committed to staying with the company. I told him where he could stick those jobs and the precious company. I may live to regret that decision but things would have to get pretty bad for me to mourn walking out on that shower.

Officially they have to give me a month's notice before they make me redundant. I am supposed to work up until that point, but I can't see myself going in to the office much over the coming month.

Looking on the bright side, I can stay up and watch the

remaining World Cup games without having to get up first thing in the morning and trek off to work. And losing my job must put me slightly closer to achieving my goal of getting a more interesting job. But with less than three months to go until my 43rd birthday, I am still way off getting a new life. I have taken some positive steps over the past few months but there is every chance that, come my birthday, I will be unemployed, in rent arrears and feeling sorry for myself as my kids jet off to exotic places with Mr comb-over or whatever new fancy man's name is.

Thursday 3rd July

Last night I turned my alarm off. Bollocks to going into work. Half an hour later I changed my mind and set the alarm for 6am. This morning, by the time I stopped for breakfast I had completed one job application and started another. Remember, shit happens to those that let shit happen. Maybe I should write my own self-help book?

I had another row with my ex on the phone this evening. The summer months are the time of year when hurricanes can hit the Caribbean.

'Don't you think you are being irresponsible taking our kids to Antigua in the hurricane season?' I asked her.

'Mark says the villa is very well built and would survive a hurricane,' she replied. Oh, Mark says, does he? Well, that's alright then.

'I don't give a shit whether the villa survives,' I told her, 'it's my children I am worried about.'

I don't know what I was hoping to achieve through this conversation but inevitably I didn't achieve it. They are still going to Antigua.

Friday 4th July

I couldn't be bothered to go to work today either. This was a conscious, proactive decision, not a wallowing-in-self-pity one. Honestly. Despite me not going in, there were still some developments on the work front. Michelle, head of HR, phoned and asked me to come in on Monday for a chat. I don't think she was just ringing to bollock me for not showing up at work since I was told I didn't get my job. I need to hand my work phone back and pick some personal stuff up anyway so I agreed to go in.

In other developments, I got a letter from the estate agent 'reminding' me that I am not allowed to keep pets in my flat. Great. I must admit I didn't actually read the tenancy agreement before signing it. What can I say? I am not giving Albus away. After thinking long and hard about the situation I did the sensible thing and gave the letter to Albus to chew up.

I am struggling to stay positive at the moment. I must remember that shit happens to those that let shit happen to them.

Sunday 6th July

Yesterday night I went to a dinner party hosted by Julia, aka Miss Putney. This was the follow-up to the dinner I went to in April at Katie and Bryan Green's house. I had totally forgotten about it until about lunchtime yesterday when Julia phoned me to check I was going. 'Of course, I'll be there,' I replied. I had nothing better to do as the kids were otherwise occupied and Amy was away in Saffron Walden with friends. The invitation gave me something to do on a Saturday night.

The same six people were there again. Katie and Bryan who the boys and I are going away with in a few weeks, John and Tracey, and Julia and myself. I arrived at the door of Julia's modern house just off the back of Putney High Street with some apprehension. After the week I have had I could do with a good night out, but I did wonder what I was doing there without Amy. At the first dinner party at Katie and Bryan's in Southfields, the hosts had unashamedly invited Julia and me as their two single friends. If their intention was to matchmake, it didn't quite work. I am now with Amy so things are different. Or at least they should have been.

It turned out to be a memorable evening. The company, the wine and the food were all top notch although I must admit I am getting a bit bored with spag bol now, even when someone else cooks it better than me. Julia had gone to great lengths to doll herself and her house up. There were flowers or candles on every surface, and some surfaces had both. Neither did my asthma any good.

Unfortunately for me, we spent half the evening talking about my employment situation. Bryan is a lawyer and Katie a recruitment consultant. Bryan wanted to sue the bastards for constructive dismissal whereas Katie took pleasure in telling me straight that I was not very appointable and nothing about me stood out to potential new employers except maybe for my big nose. I am apparently 'practically unappointable' at the moment because I have been with one company for ten years and in a niche job with few transferrable skills. That made me feel better.

To solve this problem, Katie recommended that I 'reinvent' myself.

'How do I do that?' I asked.

'Easy. You lie more imaginatively on your CV.' Her ideas for 'making me more marketable' included inventing some interesting voluntary work, thinking of some rewarding things you could do on a self-employed basis and claiming you have done them, and bribing a few people in professional-sounding jobs to act as your referees on job applications.

Even John and Tracey joined in. Tracey is a hairdresser and told me she hadn't seen my hairstyle since she cut Peter Beardsley's hair twenty years ago. John is a local politician and thinks I have the right experience to go into politics. I don't know how he knew I had been fiddling my expenses for years. I suspect that Katie and Bryan will take great delight in continuing this conversation in Turkey.

Having had dinner at Katie and Bryan's and now at Julia's, it was agreed that it was my turn to host next. A date of 3rd September was entered into various smartphones at the end of the evening. I am not sure everyone will fit into my Morden flat but I didn't protest because I like the idea of hosting a dinner party. I haven't done it for a while.

Anyway, I wish I could say that the evening ended on a convivial note with us all going off in our respective directions and that's that. Unfortunately we didn't all go off home. I feel crap about what actually happened but in my defence I was feeling low. Losing my job was a real kick to my self-esteem. The dissection of my future career prospects hadn't helped my feel-good factor either. By the end of the dinner party I was feeling pretty depressed and a little bit drunk.

So when Julia put her hand on my knee under the table as we were finishing off the cheese and biscuits, I was a bit slow to react.

Until tonight I had thought that Julia and I were only ever going to be friends. She wasn't my Amy. Even before I knew Amy, I didn't lie in bed imagining what it would be like to be with Julia. Well, not much anyway. Until last night I would have guessed that Julia felt the same level of interest, bordering on indifference, about me. But as has been noted before, I am a bit out of practice at reading the signals. I have never been in practice really. Julia had been attentive to my every need all evening but I had just put that down to her being a good hostess.

But when her hand began stroking my leg, I began to realise that she had other intentions altogether.

When my brain caught up with events, my first thought was of Amy. Amy is the one I want to be with. So why didn't I just remove Julia's hand from my leg straight away? Maybe it was the alcohol that made me slow to react. If I am being honest with myself though, there was definitely some small part of my brain telling me that after my shitty week, I wanted to be needed. Or more to the point, I needed to be wanted. I needed some physical contact.

As my internal battle with myself was raging, Julia's hand had moved from my knee to somewhere further up my leg and it was becoming increasingly hard to think straight. It was becoming increasingly hard.

There is only so much I want to say in this diary. I need to confess that my willpower deserted me totally last night. When the others went home, the metaphorical fireworks went off, accompanied by a rousing crescendo of music. The crescendo was more of recorders and triangles than trombones and bass drums, but that's about as descriptive as I am prepared to get on paper.

I came home this morning.

Reflecting on the events of last night, on the plus side there endeth the longest drought of my adult life. Julia and I were more than compatible in bed. The sex was better than anything I remember having with my ex. Even in the early stages of our relationship, I had often felt that my ex simply did what was expected of her in the bedroom. Julia, on the other hand, genuinely seemed to enjoy our nakedness and got me to do things to her that I hadn't ever done for my ex.

But I fear that the negatives of my actions outweigh the positives. My love life, or should I say my sex life, has not been particularly noteworthy up until now. I have never two-timed anyone and haven't even remotely been considered a love rat. So you should believe me when I say I am wrestling with my emotions today. I feel like a complete shit. I have cheated on Amy even before anything serious has happened between us.

Monday 7ᵗʰ July

I met Michelle from HR this morning.

To cut to the chase, it turns out that short skirt Sarah is pregnant with Daniel boss-man's child. The darling little sprog is due around Christmas time. That means they need to find someone to replace Sarah to do the job I had been doing for years. Michelle told me this over a coffee. 'What do you think about staying with us to cover Sarah's maternity leave?' she asked.

Now, the sensible answer might have been 'OK, why not.' But I have mentally moved on from my current job since being told I was going to be made redundant a couple of weeks ago. In fact I don't think I have mentally been there for years. For my own self-esteem as much as anything, I need to start something new.

I not only told Michelle where she could stick her kind offer, but I also went a step further and recited some of Bryan's arguments from Saturday night, calling into question the fairness of the original interviews.

'How can it be fair that I was interviewed by someone who was shagging the other candidate for the job?' I asked. Like I ever had a chance of getting that job. I didn't quite threaten legal action or whatever formal process I would have to go down to embarrass work and get compensation, but I think Michelle got the message. She told me that if my mind was made up about leaving, she would see what she could do to get me 'an enhanced redundancy package' in view of the circumstances.

Not a bad result, but with rent and maintenance payments to pay, I may live to regret putting my pride ahead of my wallet and not taking the offer of continuing in my job for another year or so.

I am still living to regret my actions of Saturday night. Amy texted me today suggesting we meet up for a drink one night this week. I haven't been able to bring myself to reply. I couldn't look her in the eye without her noticing a big chunk of guilt in my expression.

Wednesday 9ᵗʰ July

I have spent the last couple of days filling in application forms and feeling sorry for myself. Dave provided a welcome distraction last night when he invited me out for a beer.

Over the first few pints we concentrated on Dave's problems. It turns out that Louise only wanted rock and roll for a fortnight whilst her librarian went to study some ancient Peruvian temples. As soon as he landed back at Heathrow, Lou was there waiting for him with open arms – and open legs too according to Dave. You have to give it to her, she has got some chutzpah. Dave has now been ditched twice for a librarian. It was quite refreshing to be able to laugh at someone else's life for a change rather than him taking the piss out of mine.

We then went on to my issues. I told Dave first about Amy. He was impressed that I had found myself someone that sounded so classy. I then told him about Julia and the episode the other night.

'Bloody hell mate, I didn't think you had it in you,' was Dave's considered comment on the subject.

When I asked him what I should do about my situation, he asked me whether there was likely to be a repeat of Saturday night with Julia. 'No way,' I told him; it's Amy I want to be with, not Julia.

'Then just don't tell Amy and you'll be fine,' he advised.

I wish it were that simple. I have never really understood the term 'wrestle with your conscience' before. I do now. My conscience is beating the living daylights out of me every time I think of Saturday night.

'Chill out Graham, no one's died,' was Dave's final word on the subject as we stumbled out of the Brook at chucking out time.

The two of us were so wrapped up in our women problems that we managed to totally miss one of the most amazing football matches ever. Germany's seven-goal thrashing of Brazil totally passed us by.

Friday 11th July

They are offering me an extra month's salary 'in recognition of your exemplary commitment to the firm over the past ten years'. Well that's nice. That just about gives me enough redundancy money to live on until September. Or maybe October if I cut my maintenance payments to my ex.

The letter from Michelle also officially put me on 'gardening leave'. I thought only football managers and highly paid executives who held company secrets got put on gardening leave. But I didn't argue the toss. I'll gladly take the leave. Even if I haven't got a garden.

To celebrate receiving this letter, I wrote a goodbye email to work:

> *Hello soon-to-be-ex-colleagues,*
>
> *After ten years of paper-shuffling, I am putting the world of logistics behind me and moving on to bigger and better things. I can honestly say that I can't wait to go, and if any of you lot had any balls, you would jump too before you are pushed.*
>
> *I will not miss being required to spend half my life thinking about blue skies or what is outside a box. I am sick of cheap tea bags and can't face another stale egg mayo sandwich. Away-days are tedious beyond belief and*

appraisals aren't worth the paper they are written on. I won't miss pretending not to notice Daniel's tongue hanging out whenever Sarah walks in to the office. I didn't miss Sarah snogging Dean the post-room apprentice at last year's Christmas party.

I will, however, miss Sheena from accounts. I will miss being paid whilst spending the whole of the first half of 2012 searching online for Olympic tickets – I got loads in the end. I will miss inserting rude words into lengthy performance reports just to see if anyone actually reads them. After ten years of doing this, I can categorically say that they don't. Basically, I will miss the money. I am not sure I have earned it but it has come in useful.

Don't bother writing a card or having a collection. I never put a penny into your birthday, wedding or new baby cards so I wouldn't want you to have to feel you should contribute to a leaving card for me. Actually, Danny boy, I hope you don't mind but when your birthday collection came round a couple of months ago I was a bit skint at the time so I took a couple of quid out and paid for my lunch with it.

Love and kisses.
Graham

That is called burning bridges.

Sunday 13ᵗʰ July

Except for the odd sporadic visit for a cup of dad's hot chocolate or a piece of cake on their way home from a school function, the boys haven't been to the flat much in the past fortnight. They tell me they have had things on but until they came to stay this weekend I was beginning to wonder whether they were avoiding the flat. They are away with my ex next weekend too so I was determined to make the most of this weekend.

Their exams have now all finished so there was no homework to be done, no annoying distractions. The boys and I could spend some quality time together. I was thinking of dropping the dog off at my parents' and going to the beach for a day, or maybe doing something less ambitious like a trip to the cinema. When I asked the boys what they wanted to do, they told me they wanted to paint their bedroom. 'It's boring, dad,' Jack explained. 'Who wants to live in a dirty grey bedroom?' Maybe the flat was the reason I hadn't seen much of them after all.

After a bit of debate over colours, the boys couldn't agree on a uniform colour scheme so I nipped out to the shops and picked up two pots of paint. Jack is painting his half of the room sea blue. Sean opted for a virtually fluorescent orange. These two colours weren't meant to be used in the same room or even the same flat but so what. The landlord might moan but Albus can see him off.

More debates were had about where one half of the room stops and the other starts, but eventually we set out painting.

Lots of mess was made before the kids got the hang of how much paint to put on their respective brushes. We had some laughs along the way. Jack used his paint brush to write rude words over the wall. That was ok by me so long as the rude words were painted on Jack's own side of the room with Jack's own paint. When Sean used his orange paint to write 'Jack is a penis' on Jack's sky blue side whilst Jack and I were out of the bedroom, things became a bit problematic. It was nothing a couple of extra coats of blue as the day went on wouldn't cure though.

I was making lunch in the kitchen when I overheard a conversation between the boys in their bedroom (it isn't a big flat). Jack was telling Sean that he liked being at my place because I was happy and didn't snap at them all the time like I used to.

'It's because he is in luuuvvv,' Sean announced.

'I am not sure he is,' Jack responded. 'Lucy's mum hasn't talked to him in ages. She thinks he might have ditched her already.'

'Why would he do that?' Sean asked.

'God knows. Because he is a prat. Who knows why dad does what he does.'

Who knows indeed. Who knows why I slept with Julia. Who knows why I haven't pulled my finger out and phoned Amy. Actually I know. It is because I am ashamed of myself. But as Dave said, no one died. I need to get over it and move on. I left the chicken sandwiches half-made and went into my bedroom and phoned Amy.

I wasn't sure I was capable of saying anything trivial without giving my indiscretion away so I launched straight in when she answered. 'Do you fancy going away somewhere with me next weekend?' No 'hello', no 'sorry I haven't phoned.'

'Are you offering to take me on a dirty weekend, Mr Hope?' Amy asked.

'No, er, um…' I stuttered.

'That's a shame, I quite fancy the idea myself,' she said. It turns out that Lucy's dad is taking Lucy to Paris for the weekend to see some horse-related show so my timing was ideal. My parents used to take me to Bognor Regis if I was lucky.

I went back to making the chicken sandwiches with a smile on my face.

The boys are staying with me until school tomorrow. They wanted to watch the world cup final with me. Argentina, my sweepstake pick, played Germany. Germany won which didn't bother me too much because I couldn't have faced making another trip in to work just to pick up my sweepstake winnings.

Tuesday 15th July

So the destinations on the short-list for the dirty weekend were Bournemouth or Ambleside in the Lake District. I suggested Bournemouth because it is nearer and cheaper but Amy turned her nose up at spending a weekend away from her daughter in a place that would be teeming with kids. Fair enough. So Ambleside it is.

It occurred to me today that I had better do some shopping before we go. There was a little detail that I didn't share last week about my encounter with Julia. When she was ripping my clothes off, she nearly changed her mind when she saw my 'off-white', fraying and saggy underwear. To be fair, I wasn't anticipating having to display my Tesco three-for-a-fiver briefs to anyone else. It didn't put Julia off for long but I don't want to take the same chance with Amy.

My ex used to buy all of my underwear and I don't think I have bought any nightclothes since, well, ever. So off I went to M&S (surely one step up from Tesco?). I thought about asking Dave whether I should go for briefs or boxers but he would have told all my mates down the pub so I decided not to go down that route. I even went as far as to google men's underwear fashion before I went but I was still none the wiser about which I should go for. In the end I opted for briefs – large, of course, as I couldn't bring myself to go up to the pretty shop assistant holding anything other than large.

Wednesday 16th July

The boys came to see me this evening because my ex had to work late.

I was in the kitchen washing up when Jack called to me from the front room. 'Dad, is there something you want to tell us?'

'What do you mean, is there something I want to tell you?'

'You know, about your sex life?'

That stopped me in my tracks. What could Jack mean? Julia? Or maybe going away with Amy this weekend?

'I can't think of anything I want to tell you about my sex life, son,' I said in as calm a voice as I could muster as I walked in to the front room to see what the boys were on about.

'Did you split up with mum because you are gay?' Jack asked. Where had that come from?

'No, I am not gay,' I responded, 'whatever gave you that idea?'

'Well, your sister is gay, and I just found these pictures of buff men in their underwear on your browser on your phone.'

I took the phone from my son. He was looking at my Google search for men's underwear. I sighed with relief as I explained to him that I was buying new pants. Amy and I had elected not to tell our respective children about our planned dirty weekend. At that point I was glad that Jack didn't make the connection between my new underwear and my attempts to please Amy.

My boys and I had take-away pizzas for dinner – the ones Jack was supposed to be ordering when he was using my phone.

Friday 18th –
Monday 21st July

My dirty weekend with Amy didn't go exactly as I had planned.

I was quite nervous about the whole thing. Other than a few evenings drinking and a few strolls with our dogs, Amy and I hadn't spent much time together before this weekend. We had only kissed a couple of times. I haven't even been to her house. She hasn't been to my flat either but I don't mind that. Maybe it was a bit soon to be going on a dirty weekend?

Would I be able to hide my guilt from my adulterous escapade? Would we get on? Would we have enough to say to each other? OK, maybe those things weren't at the forefront of my mind. Would the sex be any good? Could I keep going for more than a minute? Would I manage more than once a day? Would we even have sex?

All these questions were bouncing around in my head as we travelled up to the Lake District in Amy's Porsche. I am not a real petrol-head but what bloke wouldn't look forward to travelling in a Porsche? Amy even let me drive. Driving the Porsche made driving in my crappy old people carrier feel like steering a motor scooter through treacle. A couple of times I had to put the brakes on quickly because I hadn't anticipated the power of the acceleration.

My driving experience didn't last long though. My contact lens blew out on the A3 so we had to settle for roof up and Amy driving the rest of the way. That wasn't exactly the most auspicious start to the weekend. And things got worse as the M something-or-other was an effing nightmare. We were aiming to find a nice country pub somewhere a fair way north of Birmingham to have lunch. In the end we had to settle for a service station snack.

When we eventually arrived at the bed and breakfast, our first impressions were good. The view was spectacular. But that is about the best that can be said for the B&B. The worst that can be said for it is that the room only had twin beds. And they creaked, even when you just sat on them.

'Do you want me to moan?' Amy asked.

Yes, yes, yes. It took me a while to work out that Amy meant complain to the manager about the twin beds.

In any event, by this point I wasn't feeling exactly horny. In fact I was feeling decidedly dodgy. Was it nerves? I don't think so. Nerves imply butterflies in your stomach. What I had in my stomach felt more like flesh-eating reptiles. I blame the pasty I had picked up from the service station. Maybe they should tax them more?

My first night with Amy should have been a thing of beauty. Instead I spent most of it trying to be discreet whilst throwing up or worse in the toilet. Amy was almost certainly glad of the twin beds in the end. She was also glad she had chosen a cheese sandwich rather than the pasty.

I was still feeling fragile in the morning and we were a bit late going down to breakfast. On walking in to the dining room, we were somewhat surprised to be given a standing ovation by a group of blokes sitting in the corner. A tad self-consciously we waved to them and got on with choosing our fruit juices – actually, water for me, on account of my dodgy stomach.

The establishment's proprietor, a buxom old goat with a

mischievous grin on her face, wandered over and asked us for our breakfast order. Once we had put in our requests she whispered to us conspiratorially. 'Do you know, I haven't seen the chandelier wobble like that since the vicar and his wife came to stay in 1985.'

'What are you talking about?' I asked.

'Say no more, say no more,' she said with a nod and a wink.

A few minutes later a clinically obese couple waddled in for breakfast looking rather red-faced but contented. I pushed my solitary piece of toast aside and gave up on breakfast.

Amy made a decent job of hiding her irritation at being called on to be a nursemaid rather than a lover for the first day of our trip. Instead of tackling Helvellyn and Striding Edge we ended up sitting in tea rooms and putting our world to rights. 'Do you know, you're the most gorgeous person I have ever spent the night with in the Lake District,' I told her.

'How many people have you spent the night with in the Lakes before?' she asked.

'Never mind that,' I told her.

'Do you know, Mr Hope, you are the only man who has managed to keep me awake all night on a dirty weekend,' Amy responded with her tongue firmly stuck in her cheek.

With my recovery almost complete, we decided to walk to Troutbeck and have an early dinner in a pub. Our kids and dogs would have loved the walk but I confess I was quite happy without any unnecessary distractions.

We had a very pleasant early pub dinner. I ordered a jacket potato, the blandest thing I could find on the menu. As the bill arrived Amy went off for a loo break. Convenient timing. Anyway, whilst I got my credit card out I took the opportunity to give myself another pep-talk. 'Come on Graham, pull yourself together. Get a grip and start showing your kahunas, metaphorically speaking at least. Think Ben

Affleck not Benny Hill; Billy Crystal not Billy no mates; George Clooney not George and Zippy. At the moment you are Hugh Grant without the charm or the looks – i.e. nothing. Come on, man up.' Churchillian stuff, even if I do say so myself.

'Darling, I am feeling much better now,' I announced as Amy returned from the ladies. 'Why don't we take a scenic walk back to our room and then see if we can stay awake all night for the right reasons?'

'Sorry Graham,' Amy replied, looking disappointed, 'I have just discovered Aunt Flo has come to visit earlier than I had expected.'

'Aunt Flo? When? You didn't say anything about an Auntie visiting us in the Lakes?' I was confused by this unexpected development.

'Aunt Flo, my time of the month. It must have been all that walking,' Amy clarified. I probably blushed slightly at that point. Another difference between my ex and Amy is that my ex called a spade a spade. She would warn me that her period was coming. Mind you, my ex didn't need to warn me because her mood swings gave me all the warning I needed.

Instead of a night of unrestrained passion, Amy and I shared a single bed. We did continue to get acquainted with each other but I won't go in to details.

Yesterday was a relaxing day. We spent it strolling around quaint little villages with the million other tourists. We must now be famous in Asia, having appeared in the background of hundreds of Japanese tourists' photos. In some ways, removing any possibility that we were going to have sex on our trip helped us, or at least me, to relax more on the final day of our stay.

All in all, despite the earth not moving, Amy and I had a

great few days away. Amy is great fun to be with. I feel like I have known her for years. I will miss her when she and Lucy fly off on their holidays on Wednesday. I also think I was a bit harsh when I likened her to Spurs. After spending more time with her this weekend, I am now thinking Liverpool at least.

Wednesday 23rd July

Amy and Lucy jetted off to visit Amy's sister in San Diego this lunchtime. Her ex was supposed to take them to the airport but he let them down at the last minute so I stepped in. I will do anything to get in to Amy's good books, especially if it gives me the chance to give her a last kiss goodbye before she flies. I will miss her.

Jack will apparently miss Lucy too. He begged me to let him come to the airport. It was his final day of school before the holidays. I would have probably said yes but my ex would have thrown a wobbly so I told him he couldn't come. According to Amy, Lucy's dad had moaned at his daughter at the weekend because despite being in Paris, she spent the whole time texting Jack. She was on her phone all the way to the airport today too.

My dad has reached the ripe old age of 70. Actually 70 isn't particularly ripe and old, or at least it doesn't seem so to me now that I am nearly two thirds of the way there myself, but to my kids their granddad is really old. To celebrate the momentous occasion, he invited his two children to dinner.

As I set off on the short walk from my flat to my parents' house, I saw Jack, still in his school uniform, cycling across Martin Way on his way home to his mum. I crossed over to meet him. Before I even reached him I could tell he wasn't happy. 'What's up soldier?' I asked by way of greeting.

'Nothing dad,' he mumbled. He wouldn't make eye contact with me which, in my experience, is a sure sign that there is something up.

'How come you're so late leaving school? I thought you were supposed to finish early on your last day.'

'I got another stupid detention,' Jack admitted, still not looking at me. Once I had got the thumbscrews out, I got Jack to admit that he had been caught hiding in the toilets texting Lucy when he should have been in a maths lesson. 'They were only watching a bloody DVD in maths,' Jack moaned.

'Son, you are too young to be that obsessed with a girl,' I told him. I didn't bother getting too stroppy with him about his behaviour in school because it is the last day of term and if Amy's prediction is anything to go by, Lucy and Jack might not be together when school starts up again in September.

As I arrived at my parents', my sister Hilary and her partner Donna were just taking their first sips of Prosecco. 'Sorry I'm late,' I announced as I let myself in with the key I hadn't got around to returning.

The evening was just like old times. My mum and dad, with able support from Hills, cans of London Pride and bottles of Prosecco, spent the evening reminding me that I am not only divorced but jobless. My mum had 'inadvertently' opened a letter addressed to me from my current employer giving me formal notice of my redundancy.

'Oh, and I saw your ex the other day in Wimbledon. She told me she has got a new fellow. A stockbroker or something like that, isn't he?' my mum asked. My ex would have taken great pleasure in showing my mum that she was doing better without me thank you very much.

'So what, I have got a new woman too,' I boasted before I could stop myself. I hadn't intended to tell my family about Amy but I couldn't just sit there and be ritually humiliated all evening.

'Have you? Isn't it a bit soon after your divorce?' my mum asked.

'I hope you aren't setting a bad example to your children,' my dad offered.

'Is she fit?' was my dear sister's contribution. Thankfully, Donna didn't feel she knew me well enough to chip in.

By the time I scrunched up my last can and threw it into the recycling, I had promised to bring Amy over to meet my parents. Me and my big mouth.

Friday 25th July

Jack and Sean were hyper this evening. They are with me from now until we get back from Turkey. It feels good. We went off to buy some summer clothes. Why is it that whatever the weather, all the kids want is khakis? Will someone tell them there isn't a war on in Turkey?

I can't wait to be solely responsible for my boys for more than just the odd day or two. I have been looking forward to this holiday since the moment Katie and Bryan invited us. It will be the longest continuous spell of time I have had with Jack and Sean since the two weeks I spent with them last summer when my ex buggered off to some Scottish island to 'find herself'. I don't know what she found but when she came back she told me she wanted the divorce.

The three of us got on fine over that two week period, although we didn't do much other than enjoy relaxing in a house with no tense atmosphere and no excessive rules. I wouldn't have had the confidence to take the boys abroad without my ex this time last year so our trip to Turkey should definitely be seen as a step forward in my quest to get a life.

Sunday 27th July – Sunday 3rd August

Maybe we should have stayed at home. I thought beach-based holidays in Turkey were supposed to be full of sun-bathing and water-based fun, with the added bonus of a bit of lager-supping thrown in. I thought they were supposed to be put-your-feet-up-type holidays during which families bonded and made memories. Well, I suppose we did make memories.

Our fun started at Gatwick as we arrived for our early morning flight. I have heard it said that you don't truly get to know people until you go on holiday with them. Well, I felt like I knew Katie and Bryan too well by the time we reached passport control. They were rowing when we met them at the check-in desk. The first thing I heard Katie say to Bryan as we approached their group with open arms ready to give them a start-of-holiday bear hug was, 'For fuck's sake Bryan, I can't believe you forgot to pack the vodka. You know I need a few drinks to calm my nerves before I get on the plane.'

Despite Katie buying a replacement bottle in duty free, she still wasn't happy. 'Where the hell is my makeup bag? You didn't put it in the suitcase did you? For fuck's sake, you are a stupid man.' Bryan looked at me apologetically and shrugged.

Luckily whilst most of this was going on Jack and Sean were in an amusement arcade with Josh and Theo, the Green's children. I am no prude but I was glad that the boys weren't exposed to the worst of Katie's language. I had brought them on holiday to forget family strife, not to share other people's.

Sometimes when you spend the odd evening with a couple, you think things like 'ah, aren't they the perfect couple' and 'oh, they look so happy together'. I am sure my ex and I used to say that sort of thing about Katie and Bryan. How wrong we were. As we were boarding the plane, Katie grabbed Josh and Theo and threatened to take them home again if Bryan didn't apologise for some insult or other I didn't quite catch. Bryan just walked on to the plane and eventually Katie and the kids followed.

I am fully up for a pint or two at the airport whatever time our holiday flight is, but I have never gone to the extreme that Katie did on our journey to Turkey. She carried on drinking on the plane and was virtually comatose by the time we had landed in Turkey. At least she slept in the taxi to the villa. Her outbursts were limited to the odd belch, an infrequent snore and a slightly more regular fart. I was charitable at the time and put this all down to the stress of her job or of travelling or something like that.

When we arrived at our villa we were really pleased with what we saw. Our home for the week was a huge whitewashed house, set into the mountainside just above Ovacik, a small town a few miles inland from Oludeniz. My ex would have loved the view, especially the sunset over the mountains.

Inside the villa, there were four large bedrooms, two with en suites. Outside, there was a balcony to the front with views over the surrounding mountains and, much more impor-tantly to the children, the rear of the villa housed a large pool. Much more importantly to Katie, there was a bar area and large fridge next to the pool. The first thing Katie and Bryan did when we got to the villa was stock up the bar from the local supermarket.

There were times during our holiday where I really found myself missing my ex. We had some great family holidays. That first night, after Katie's exploits on the journey to the villa, I sat by the pool after everyone else had gone to bed and felt a little bit homesick. My ex would have loved sitting there with me, drinking a chilled glass of wine and watching the stars gradually emerge in the darkening sky.

My ex would also have known how best to shield the kids from Katie's worst excesses. I struggled with that bit. Katie and Bryan carried on arguing throughout our first full day at the villa. Not unconnected, Katie carried on drinking too. She didn't seem to care who was around her either. At one point, the kids' human pyramid in the pool collapsed and Katie got soaked in the resulting splash. 'For fuck's sake you lot, can't you go and play somewhere else?' she shouted at the four of them.

I was about to lose the plot with Katie when Bryan put his hand out and stopped me. 'Leave it to me, Graham,' he said, pleading with his eyes for me to let him handle things. I hurriedly took all four kids off to the beach, bought them ice creams and, at least on the surface, they seemed to forget about Katie's outburst. Even at the height of our divorce, my ex and I didn't speak to our children like that. I sat on a sunbed with my feet in the tranquil waters of the Blue Lagoon, feeling pretty disconsolate. I had brought my children here to get away from family strife, only to drop them smack bang in the middle of something far more vitriolic than they had previously experienced.

I don't know what I would have done if Katie had carried on with her excessive drinking and obnoxious outbursts throughout the holiday. Thankfully, whatever Bryan said while the four kids and I were at the beach seemed to calm Katie down for the next couple of days at least.

Our third full day was actually pretty harmonious. We all went to the beach, hired kayaks, raced each other and played games like 'last man standing in their boat wins an ice cream'. Katie, who had noticeably cut down on her drinking, even joined in. It turned out that balance wasn't her strong point even when she was sober.

In the afternoon, the adults chilled out on sunbeds as the kids continued their water games. I even got in a spot of bird watching. At least when I was married I could hide behind my mirrored sunglasses, eye up the talent on display on the beach and know that when I felt horny, assuming she was up for it I could go back to the villa with the wife. Now I don't have that luxury.

The seven of us finished off our day with a traditional Turkish meal. The adults enjoyed the belly dancing and fire dancing even if the kids were less than impressed.

The next couple of days were just as good. We visited a few different beaches, mostly in the lagoon. The older boys jumped off rock faces in to the sea and generally they laughed a lot. The adult conversation never really flowed, though.

As the days progressed, Katie slipped back into her drinking habit. The results were predictable. On the fifth evening, the seven of us went to Seahorse Beach to have dinner on the beach. It was one of the most picturesque settings I had ever eaten at. The sun was setting across the other side of the lagoon. The shimmering water was lapping the sand only feet from where we sat. We shared this view with one other couple who had booked the same treatment as us. Poor them.

Katie was pretty plastered by the time our dinner was served. She argued with the waiter about which swordfish steak she had ordered. At least I think that was what she was saying in her alcohol-induced slur. I could see Bryan visibly fretting about what she was going to say or do next. He was right to fret. As she stood up to continue her argument with the waiter, she stumbled forwards and landed face first on the table, sending plates and drinks crashing on to the sand.

None of us fancied staying after Katie's performance so we paid the bill and left, apologising as we went for spoiling the other couple's enjoyment of the otherwise peaceful scene. Ironically, as we left the beach, a wedding ceremony was starting up on the next beach along.

Once we got back to the villa, I took the boys out to the table by the pool for a pre-bed game of cards. Unfortunately, Katie insisted on coming out to the poolside bar to have one last drink.

After downing her latest glass of wine, she once again stumbled out of her chair and asked Bryan to take her to bed. The kids witnessed the encounter.

'You go to bed Katie, but I am not coming with you. You are too drunk,' Bryan told his wife.

Katie, in the most ungainly manner possible and in full view of the kids, lifted her skirt and clambered on to Bryan's lap, facing him with her legs sticking out over the arms of the plastic chair. 'Bryan, I haven't had a fuck in months because you've been too busy shagging that tarty hairdresser to notice me.'

'You haven't had a fuck in months because you are an ugly cow, not because I have been shagging that tarty hairdresser,' Bryan responded.

At that point I intervened for the sake of the children and suggested quite forcibly that Katie and Bryan might want to carry on their conversation in private.

'Oh fuck off Graham,' Katie shouted, 'even you have had sex more recently than me so you can shut the fuck up too.'

'God,' Jack joined in, 'Dad hasn't had sex since he split up with mum and that's, like, ages ago.'

'Yes he has, he shagged Julia after her dinner party,' Katie responded.

'Who the fuck's Julia?' Twelve-year-old Sean asked.

I don't know how my sex life managed to get worked into an argument between Katie and Bryan, but the fact is that it did. They say 'never go to bed on an argument'. As no one was prepared to talk to anyone after Katie and Bryan's outburst, including my kids to me, we all went to bed.

The following day, Bryan went home. Or at least he left the villa. Katie was quiet all day. I am not sure she could even remember the events of the night before. She apologised at lunchtime. I was preparing our baguettes and mumbled my acceptance of her apology.

'Do you think I am attractive?' she asked.

I think she was just seeking reassurance after Bryan called her an ugly cow but thinking that I needed to avoid giving off misleading signals, I simply shook my head. Things were even quieter in the afternoon.

I hate my children witnessing adults behaving so badly. I failed in my duty as a father to shield them. I tried repeatedly to talk to the boys. Not just my two but Josh and Theo too. I couldn't help thinking that Josh and Theo had heard all this before. If there is some small consolation to be taken from Katie and Bryan's antics it is that my children might be living in a broken home but they have never heard their parents disrespect each other to that extent.

Of all the children, Sean seemed to have been the least affected by the argument. He carried on playing his swimming pool games despite the others being less willing to join in. He said the 'F' word in the argument but I didn't have the energy, let alone the moral currency, to pull him up for that.

I have already beaten myself up over my exploits with Julia. The evening after Katie's outburst, Jack decided he wanted his turn. I can't say I blame him. 'How could you do such a thing, dad?' he asked. The only way of responding to Jack was to be honest with him. I didn't try to justify my sleeping with Julia but I did explain the circumstances that led to me making the wrong choice.

'Do you love Julia?' he asked.

'No.'

'Do you love Amy?'

'Love's a hard thing to define,' I told him.

'I love Lucy,' Jack confessed.

I tried to talk to Jack about his declaration of love for Lucy but, unlike a month ago when he actively sought out my advice on the subject of girls, this time he didn't want to listen.

Until now I have always striven to maintain a fairly traditional set of boundaries in my relationship with my sons. I try to be someone they can look up to and respect. Someone they can trust to know the right thing to do, someone who will always do the right thing. After recent events it will take me a while to win back their trust and respect.

I can't blame Jack for being annoyed with me. He was still annoyed even after I had talked to him. I am not setting the right example to my kids. I don't think he has texted the news to Lucy but I can't bring myself to ask him outright. If only I had taken Julia's hand off my leg at that dinner party.

Our final full day in Turkey was no less eventful that those that had gone before it. I had become the responsible adult for all four children. Katie spent the day doing god knows what at the villa. The four children and I went to the beach. We did all the traditional stuff, from the banana boat (I fell off but the kids stayed on), to ice-creams and digging holes in the sand. We were out in the sun all day.

As it was our last night in Turkey and despite me already having blown my holiday budget, I took the four boys out to dinner. I was hoping for a good Turkish meze and maybe a bit more belly dancing but after the last couple of days I decided to let the kids choose the restaurant. Burgers and chips it was then. We had a reasonable night. It amazes me how resilient kids are.

When we returned to the villa, I was knackered and wanted my bed but the kids wanted to have one last competition of jumping into the pool as spectacularly as possible. I succumbed and joined in with them. Sean tried to jump off a plastic chair. The chair slipped as he as jumping and Sean's heel landed on the edge of the pool step. He was in agony.

After waking Katie up from her drunken stupor and leaving her in charge of the other three kids (even when pissed she couldn't do a worse job than me), off I went with Sean to hospital.

To cut a long story short (because I am tired and haven't slept for 36 hours) we were at the hospital all night. They X-rayed Sean's ankle. A doctor tried to talk to me about what they wanted to do to fix it but his grasp of English, although admittedly infinitely better than my grasp of Turkish, wasn't sufficient for me to comprehend what he was talking about. At one point they were trying to ask me about insurance. It turns out that the stupid little health insurance cards I had so diligently applied for before we went on holiday aren't valid in Turkey.

As dawn approached, I decided it would be easier to get Sean home to London. I carried him out of the hospital, back to the villa, chucked our stuff into suitcases, carried them and Sean to the airport, onto the plane, off the plane, through the airport and straight to accident and emergency.

And that's not the end of the disasters. Jack, Josh and Theo all felt like shit during our journey home. It was probably sun stroke from yesterday as I don't remember insisting that they cream up.

I phoned my ex from the hospital waiting room. She was there in half an hour.

'What the hell were you doing?' she asked me once she had given Sean a cuddle.

I was too tired to argue. I just put my hands up and walked off to find a coffee machine. Had I hung around, I haven't got a clue what I would have said in my defence. I would have had one less leg to stand on than Sean.

When I returned from the canteen, the consultant was with my ex. Sean has broken the calcaneus bone (his heel). That's the end of his cricket season for this year, not to mention his chances of swimming in the Caribbean sea. The good news, though, is that he doesn't need surgery.

'You do know you have wrecked Sean's Antigua holiday now, don't you?' my ex muttered angrily at me as she was pushing Sean out of the hospital doors in a wheelchair.

It was an accident that could have happened to anyone, but I don't think I will enter myself for dad of the year this year.

Monday 4th August

Sean had his foot put in plaster today.

Despite everything, Jack phoned me this afternoon and thanked me for taking them on holiday. Bryan also texted me and asked if I fancied going for a beer. I am not sure I can face seeing any more of either Bryan or Katie for a while.

With less than seven weeks until my 43rd birthday, I spent today reassessing my priorities. I have made progress on some of the goals I set for myself when my divorce came through. Our Turkey trip shows that I have got some way to go before I can call myself a great dad. The Julia incident could prove my undoing with Amy. And I haven't got a job of any description, let alone a more interesting one.

On reflection, I feel the need to restate and slightly refine my goals:

1. Be a good dad;
2. Be proud of myself; and
3. Get a job

On the subject of goal three, I have spent most of today revising my CV. Did you know I once did voluntary work for the World Wildlife Fund saving tigers in India? Oh, and I ran my own health and safety business too. Katie would be proud of me.

Thursday 7th August

Getting a job has to be a real priority. The more I think about money, the more I am starting to worry. My flat might not be something I am proud of but the thought of having to move back in to my parents' fills me with dread. I have filled in five application forms over the course of the last few days. At least one of them, for a 'performance manager' job for my local council, sounds right up my street. Literally. It is based at the end of Martin Way, about a five minute walk from my flat.

Amy and Lucy arrived back from San Diego this morning. Amy's ex managed to get his arse in gear this time and picked them up from the airport. I haven't been able to get Amy out of my head since our weekend in the Lakes. Spending some quality time alone with her is even higher up my priority list than getting a job, so I was pleased when Amy phoned me when she got home and invited me to dinner at her place tomorrow night. Our kids were both supposed to be with their other parent but when Lucy and Jack got their heads together, they pleaded with us to be invited to dinner too. So now a romantic twosome has turned in to a slightly awkward foursome. I did invite Sean as well. He politely declined saying he didn't want to sit there all night and watch his brother behaving like a sissy.

Saturday 9ᵗʰ August

I am not sure if a rule book has been written for joint dates between fathers and sons and mothers and daughters, but in the taxi on the way over to Amy's, Jack and I agreed to adhere to a number of rules. Jack undertook not to mention Julia under any circumstances. I agreed to buy Jack a new games console for Christmas. Jack also made me agree:

1. Not to mention him wetting the bed when he was six or putting his mother's bikini on when he was seven
2. Not to get my phone out and show Lucy the video of him singing 'If I Only Had a Brain' in his primary school's production of the Wizard of Oz
3. Not to make him eat all his vegetables at dinner, especially if it's spinach
4. Not to boast about his academic abilities again
5. Not to kiss Amy in front of him
6. Not to laugh, comment or even look if he kisses Lucy
7. Not to pretend I am cooler than I actually am

As the taxi pulled up outside Amy's, the driver muttered, 'Bloody hell, they must be minted.' Indeed they must be. The massive iron gates were open, revealing a house adorned with stone pillars and huge windows. Secluded lighting in the gardens that lined the drive lit up a positive zoo of ornately carved animals. And unlike the gravel out the back of my flat, Amy's gravel wasn't threadbare and littered with cat shit. It looked like it had been carefully raked by a gardener just before our arrival.

On seeing the double-fronted mock something-or-other house, I half expected the butler to come rushing out to take our coats. Or is that the doorman's job? If there is a butler or a doorman, Amy must have given them the night off because she and Lucy both came to greet us. Amy and I had an awkward moment where we didn't know whether or not to kiss in front of our children and instead stuck to smiling at each other. Lucy on the other hand had no such qualms and wrapped her arms around Jack so tightly that she nearly suffocated the poor boy. I quite envied their uninhibited embrace.

Amy led us all in to her palace. I nudged Jack to get him to take his shoes off at the door but Amy laughed and told me not to be so stupid. I bet the hall carpet cost more than all the floor surfaces in my flat put together. It was about the same size too. I caught myself wondering whether it was a shag pile. We walked through to a wood-panelled dining room. The whole room was clad in dark wood. To my untrained eye it all looked a bit imposing and austere but I am sure it oozed class. The table was laid for four but big enough to host double that comfortably.

Overall the evening went well. Amy is a top cook. We had home-made spinach and ricotta calzone. Jack didn't seem to notice the spinach. After dinner, the kids adjourned to somewhere else in the house (probably the drawing room) whilst Amy and I stayed seated at the table and shared most of a bottle of claret between us.

Amy told me about her and Lucy's San Diego holiday. It wasn't as hot as they were expecting but unlike our trip to Turkey, they had no dramas to report. Lucy brought Jack back a cuddly panda as a present. If I had given Jack a panda, he would have given it to Albus and told me he wasn't a baby anymore. But apparently it is OK to receive a cuddly panda from your girlfriend.

The kids are off to Antigua tomorrow. Jack told me on the way home from Amy's that he didn't want to go. Secretly that made me feel good but I was ever the professional divorced dad and told him he would have a great time with his mum and his brother, and his mum's new bloke. 'Mark's a dork, and Sean's a cripple at the moment so I don't see how it is going to be fun,' replied Jack. The fact that Jack thinks that Mr comb-over is a dork pleased me, but I suspect the real reason that Jack didn't want to go is because he will miss Lucy.

The extent of Jack's interest in Lucy is beginning to worry me. He is living life and that is great. Being in love is exciting, exhilarating. I am not worried about them having sex or anything like that either. They are still embarrassed about getting to first base.

What worries me is how Jack will be when, and in my mind it is when and not if, he and Lucy break up. He has never had his heart broken before. I know it is something he will have to deal with at some point. I certainly did when I was a teenager – Andrea Hollingwood, I still haven't forgiven you. But as his dad I want to protect him for as long as possible. I guess I just have to accept that some things are out of my control. Jack has to live his life, heartbreak and all.

Monday 11th August

I went to my ex's this morning to see the boys off. I haven't seen Sean since he left the hospital with my ex. When I arrived he was sitting on the sofa with his foot up. He was totally grumpy and wasn't looking forward to the holiday either. I can't say I blame him. He will struggle to walk on the sand. He can't get his cast wet so I don't quite know what he will do for three weeks in Antigua. I gave him a new hand-held gaming thingy that I picked up cheaply on eBay. It was the least I could do.

I am not going to see the boys for the next three weeks. I haven't gone that long without seeing them since they were born. I bet some people don't go three weeks without seeing their kids for the whole of their lives.

I am feeling pretty flat this evening and yes, I am blaming myself for ruining Sean's Antigua trip.

My evening gloom was interrupted by a phone call. Now, before I start on this one, in my defence I should point out that the phone reception on my mobile is dodgy in the new flat and I can't read the phone screen without my glasses. I answered the phone.

'Hello gorgeous, I have missed you,' said Amy.

'I am missing you too, sexy,' I replied.

'Ah, that's good to hear. I need you. It has been a while since we made love,' Amy said.

Hang on a minute, Amy and I haven't quite made love yet. Yet. Panic.

'Er, who is this?'

'Who do you bloody think it is?' replied a cross Julia.

I tried to recover the situation by telling her I was only joking but I don't think I got away with it.

'Are you seeing someone else?' she asked.

'No, of course not.' I tried to sound outraged.

Letting women down gently is something else I don't have much experience of. In my youth it used to be them letting me down gently. Or sometimes not so gently – Andrea Hollingwood, you have a lot to answer for. I was trying to let Julia down gently and thought it would be kinder to her to say I just wanted to be friends rather than telling her I had someone else, but I couldn't seem to find the right words.

'That's all right then,' she said. 'I have really missed you over the last few weeks. Don't you think it is great having someone special in your life again?' This was getting worse.

'Oh, Julia, you are special to me but…'

'What are you doing tomorrow night?'

'Nothing, but…'

'Good, come round to mine. See you at 7.30.'

'OK, see you then,' I mumbled.

I'm a numpty. A doofus. I tried composing a text but decided I wouldn't have been very proud of myself if I had sent it. It read, 'Sorry Julia, I just can't do this anymore. Goodbye. Graham'. It sounded more like a suicide note than an end of relationship text in any case.

Tuesday 12th August

I am still missing the boys but I feel better now because I have sorted the Julia situation out. I manned up and phoned her this morning. I told her everything. Literally everything. She started off upset but by the time I got to the 'Father and son, mother and daughter' bit of the story, she was less frosty.

'Why didn't you just tell me all this in the first place?' she asked.

'I thought you'd be upset,'

'I am a bit disappointed that I won't be getting any more nookie for a while, but it isn't as if I had fallen in love with you or anything, and come to think of it, the sex wasn't the best I have ever had,' she said. Bloody cheek. In the circumstances though, I probably deserved that dig so I let it go.

Julia went on to tell me she has been talking to Katie. Apparently Katie and Bryan's relationship has been on the rocks for a while now. Bryan has moved out and is living with his parents. That sounds familiar.

This weekend is a no-kids weekend. It is also a no-football weekend. I am not quite sure what I am going to do with my time as Amy is visiting friends in Cheshire. Why is it that when I visit friends, I go to places like Morden? Amy goes to Alderley Edge or Saffron Walden.

Wednesday 13th August

This is the furthest I have ever been away from my children. And I don't like it. On the day they flew to the Caribbean I kept looking at Twitter to check for plane crashes. I never normally give that sort of thing a thought when I am flying with the boys. At least I know they arrived safely. Jack texted me and told me 'we are here'. That is about as descriptive as I would expect Jack to get via text. They have been there two days now and I haven't heard any more.

The boys are probably sitting on a luxury yacht being skippered around some idyllic island or other by Mr comb-over whilst my ex is sunbathing naked on the poop deck. I suspect this makes me a bad father but I hope they aren't having too good a time. I am not wishing them an awful holiday. Just one that isn't better than anything I can give them. I made the mistake of confessing my feelings to my parents when I went round for a coffee this afternoon. The coffee turned in to a few cans of London Pride. My mum reminded me that being a parent isn't all about me. I should be putting Jack and Sean's interests first. Apparently being a good parent is about being there when they need me, not them being there when I need them. Trust me to have social workers for parents. For once in their lives, why can't they be on my side?

I ended up having a few beers with Bryan last night. He tells me that Katie is an alcoholic. Tell me something I don't know. Bryan's contention is that it is no wonder he is having an affair with Tracey the hairdresser.

'Which came first though, the chicken or the egg?' I asked him. He didn't seem to get my meaning and I confess I wasn't interested enough in the answer to bother pursuing it.

We spent most of the night talking about the pros and cons of living with your parents. But it must be said that over the last double whiskey we talked nonstop about what Tracey was like in bed. Very noisy apparently.

Friday 15ᵗʰ August

I have got another job interview. It is for that performance management job at Merton Council. Merton is famous for Paul, the comedian, who named himself after the council. Honestly, at least according to what I read when I started researching Merton.

The interview is next week so I will do some prep over the next few days. But for now I am off to Amy's. Generally, I hate my kids not being around but occasionally it has its advantages. Lucy is at her dad's tonight too. Is tonight the night? I shaved and put my nearly new briefs on just in case.

Sunday 17ᵗʰ August

There was a spring in my step when Amy dropped me back home this afternoon. If I could whistle I would have been whistling. I have had a good few days. And nights.

I have only had sex with one divorced woman so my study of what it is like to have sex with divorced women isn't statistically significant. But having sex with a divorced woman is different from the passionate but clumsy fumblings that characterised my experiences of sex in my youth. In my youth I would always be worrying that someone's mother would come in and interrupt us, that my condom would split or that the person I was having sex with would change her mind at any moment. Foreplay was therefore pretty absent in those days.

Sex with a divorced woman is also different from the going-through-the-routine type sex I had with my wife. Even in our early days, our marital sex was little more than functional, the aim being either to produce a baby or to shut me up.

Amy and I have both got baggage. Actually she would say she has got experience, I have got baggage. We didn't rush headlong into it. We knew we had all night. We sat on her huge leather sofa and drank wine from each other's glasses. We cuddled, we kissed, we talked about what we like and what we don't like in bed, all very reasonable stuff. We drank some more and then I nearly broke my neck carrying her up her winding stately-home-style staircase to her bedroom. It was a bloody long way.

She freshened up in the bathroom while I lay on her four-poster drinking more wine to stop the feelings of self-consciousness from creeping back in. When she opened the door of her en suite dressed in only her knickers to cover her modesty and climbed on to the bed next to me (not Spurs, not Liverpool but Manchester City. Or even Real Madrid), things just worked. They weren't rushed. Nature just took its course. It was just, what's the word, right. There was even an encore.

The following morning as I was sitting in Amy's conservatory eating a late breakfast of melon and strawberries (I am more a bacon and egg man but I went with the flow today), Amy asked me what my plans were for the day. Normally I would have spent my Saturday with the boys but they are thousands of miles away. When I told her I didn't really have any plans, she invited me to stay for a bit longer.

'But isn't Lucy coming back from her dad's?' I asked.

'Yes, but we haven't got anything to hide. She knows we are seeing each other, so why shouldn't you stay?'

I have already admitted to being slightly nervous around Lucy. This isn't because Lucy is a particularly hard character to deal with. It is just that I haven't spent any time with teenage girls and conversation with them doesn't seem to come naturally to me. But as Amy was inviting me to stay, I had to get over my awkwardness and make an effort.

But being a dad myself, I could see how Lucy's dad might feel if he heard that she was spending time at her house with Amy's new lover. One of my biggest fears when getting divorced was that my ex would meet someone else and that that man would take over my 'dad' role. Everyday dad duties like making the breakfast, asking the kids about their day when they get home from school, beating the crap out of them on the sofa when they are watching some canned laughter sitcom, telling them not to hide their peas under their knife and fork, going to football with them on Saturday mornings and watching the odd over-age film with them when their mother isn't looking would be taken over by someone other than me. I can't stand the thought of that so I was very conscious not to muscle in on Lucy's dad's role. When I mentioned this to Amy, her response was fairly dismissive.

'Graham, I am only asking you if you want to stay for another day or two. I am not asking you to move in. And besides, Lucy will probably spend the whole day in her room with her stereo on. You won't even see her.'

Lucy came home at lunchtime. I stayed right out of the way when her dad dropped her off. When I say right out of the way I mean in the front bedroom peeking through the heavy velvet curtains. He has got a Porsche too. His and hers matching cars. It irked me to see that he was a good looking guy. He reminded me of someone but I couldn't quite put my finger on who it was. He didn't get out of the car so I didn't get a good look at him.

Amy was right about Lucy. I didn't see her much all day. From what I did see of her, Lucy is a good kid. Amy tells me that she has got more teenage attitude than Jack but I didn't see any evidence of it. She didn't seem to feel awkward having me around. She asked me how Jack was enjoying his holiday. I couldn't offer anything other than that he had arrived safely. 'Oh, I know they went on a boat trip yesterday and he got embarrassed when his mum sunbathed naked,' she told me.

Over the course of the day I discovered that Lucy won't want me to take her to the football so there are no worries on that score. I refrained from beating her up on the sofa and she made her own breakfast this morning, so there weren't actually too many difficult situations for me to worry about. I don't think I crossed any boundaries but I suspect that if I was her dad I would still be pissed at me for spending the night with his ex and in the same house as his daughter.

When I eventually made my way home this afternoon, the flat seemed really quiet. I spent a few minutes tidying up. That included chucking the dirty clothes that the boys had left in their two-tone room in to the washing machine. At some point I should invite Amy to visit me but I am a bit conscious of the difference between her Wimbledon Village architectural masterpiece and my Morden ex-council flat. She has seen the outside of the flat but I haven't invited her in. I reckon it is about time I did.

Tuesday 19th August

'It's a bit small,' Amy said as we lay in bed naked.

I think she was talking about the flat but I didn't dare double check.

I had succumbed and invited her round for dinner last night. Lucy was spending a couple of days with a friend in Brighton. I spent the day buying and then using a Hoover, a duster and a toilet brush. I was dusting the bedside table when the doorbell rang. I shoved the duster and polish under the bed and went to let Amy in.

As well as cleaning the flat, I had prepared a pork and Stilton dish that my mum used to cook for the family when we were growing up. Amy seemed impressed by my culinary skills.

It didn't take long for us to end up in bed. I still can't believe I am writing that. For Amy, lying in bed and looking at the ceiling was probably preferable to looking at the dirty walls and dark recesses of my sitting room. Whatever the reason for her haste to get me in to bed, I wasn't complaining.

After a lazy breakfast this morning and further taking advantage of there being no kids at home, Amy stayed in my flat writing an article for the magazine for bored housewives while I took the dogs for a walk (yes, I had two dogs in the flat last night despite not being allowed any pets).

When I got back from the park, I got a bit of a shock. Amy was standing at the door dressed only in my England cricket shirt. It wasn't that that shocked me though. It was the fact that she was talking to my ex.

'Aren't you supposed to be in Antigua?' I asked as I climbed the last flight of stairs to the door.

'Aren't you going to introduce us?' my ex replied, acidly.

Introductions were duly made. My ex, meet Amy. Amy, meet my ex. Then my ex told me she had left me loads of messages on my mobile asking me to pick them up from the airport because they were coming home early. I hadn't turned my mobile on in ages because I didn't want my mates phoning me up and disturbing me at any vital moments.

As Amy made a swift exit for the bedroom to get dressed, my ex started berating me for letting Sean break his foot, for ruining their holiday, ruining her relationship with Mark (Mr comb-over) who had apparently refused to travel back to England with them and for generally being crap. I decided that this probably wasn't the best time to mention that I had reduced her maintenance payments while she had been away too.

I said an awkward goodbye to Amy, leaving her in the flat to gather her things together, and went back to the detached house in Surrey with my ex and gave Sean and Jack a big hug. Sean told me he was glad he was home. Jack repeated his accusation that Mark is a dork. My ex, who was standing in the doorway presumably because she wanted to overhear what her son had to say about the holiday she had arranged, didn't disagree.

I should be careful what I wish for. I didn't tell my ex but I am now feeling guilty that I didn't want the boys to have a good time.

Thursday 21st August

The drama never seems to stop. I wasn't present at today's drama but I have certainly heard about it.

Jack wanted to see Lucy after his aborted holiday. He arranged to go over and see her at her house. They were planning to go to Westfield shopping centre for some 'retail therapy'. Personally I would need some proper therapy after spending the day at Westfield. Until now I thought Jack was the same but Lucy's influence is changing him. Anyway, my ex offered to give him a lift to Lucy's. I suspect my ex wanted to get a sense of who her son was seeing, and maybe meet her mother. It didn't occur to Jack that this might cause issues.

Needless to say, when my ex saw Amy she was bemused (that's one word for it. Others might be 'fuming', 'foaming at the mouth', 'spontaneously combusting' or 'going fucking bonkers'). Jack didn't know the two women had seen each other a couple of days ago.

The first I heard of this encounter was when my ex phoned me from her hands-free in the car. She ranted at me for a full fifteen minutes – the time it took her to drive from Wimbledon Village to her detached house in Surrey. As far as I could work out from her thousand-word-a-minute monologue, she made the following salient points:

1. It is good to see that you and the boys have got your-selves a ready-made new family.
2. Why didn't you tell me you knew Jack's girlfriend?
3. What does Sean do when you and Jack are holding hands with your girlfriends, or is there another sister that Sean can have?
4. I bet you all go there for sleepovers whenever you have the kids. What sort of example are you setting to your children?
5. If you think I am accepting less maintenance from you when you are off shagging some rich bitch then you've got another thing coming. (Says she whose bloke owns a villa in Antigua. If, that is, he's still her bloke.)

I would be the first to admit that some of these points are fair enough. Why didn't I tell her? Because I knew what her reaction would be. But I know I should have told her. I hadn't even thought of some of the things she raised though. What do we do when it comes to sleepovers? I guess it will be difficult as I don't want Jack to think that because I am sleeping with Amy, he can sleep with Lucy. I am not even sure he would want to yet, but that isn't the point. And what would Sean do? I don't think I had quite realised the full implications of mine and Jack's relationships. To be fair to my ex, I know that if Jack had been seeing Mr comb-over's daughter, I would have ranted too.

Immediately after my ex finished damaging my eardrums, Amy called. She alternated from anger at the way my ex spoke to her to concern that Lucy and Jack had overheard. They shouldn't have to concern themselves with grown-up stuff, and Jack in particular tends to feel responsibility for his mother's welfare. In my book it is really important that our children don't feel responsibility for their parents. They have enough to worry about being kids. Amy was naturally a bit perturbed by this morning's events.

The third phone call I received in the space of an hour was from Jack. He was speaking quietly so I could tell he was trying to hide his call from Lucy and Amy. 'Dad,' he said, 'Mum has only given me twenty quid. I think Lucy has got fifty. Can you meet us at Wimbledon station and lend me some more money?' He was obviously deeply affected by the encounter then.

Friday 22nd August

This afternoon's big event was my latest job interview, for that council job. I got radical yesterday and bought a new suit and tie. Despite Katie's advice to push the boat out on snappy work clothing I stuck with M&S, but did go for the next price bracket up from the bargain bin.

So I turned up at the ugly 1960s office block that dwarfs the surrounding Morden terraced houses feeling quite dapper and inwardly confident. How hard could a council job be? All the papers say that public sector workers are over-paid and under-worked. Well, I could cope with that. As an added bonus I know a thing or two about performance management. And following a couple of days of research mainly spent reading lefty publications like the Guardian, I now know a thing or two about what councils do too. I have quite a few applications in for jobs at the moment but this one is the one I have really pinned my hopes on. It is a job I can do, and it is only based a five minute walk away from my flat. And the pay is on a par with what I was getting in my previous job. If I got this job, my rent payments would be manageable and I would have enough left over after paying the ex her slice to buy the kids the occasional treat.

The interviews were running late so I had to wait in a reception area for half an hour. They gave me a better quality cup of tea than I ever drank at my previous job. Who says the public sector isn't as good as the private sector?

I was interviewed by the assistant director of something, the group manager of something else and the head of human resources, the only man on the panel. First impressions were good – I was dressed smarter than them. The bloke from HR didn't even have a tie on.

I think I gave a pretty good account of myself in the interview. I had worked out that it would take about twenty houses' council tax for a year to pay my salary. Basically, at the end of each year, if I couldn't demonstrate that I had helped bring about changes that improved things or saved more than my salary, then it wasn't worth them employing me. I wasn't sure whether I had overdone it when I outlined this theory because I could see the cogs going round in the assistant director's head. She was trying to work out how many streets' council tax would pay for her salary.

They were particularly impressed with my voluntary work with the tigers and with Richard Branson being the person I put down to give me a reference.

I am feeling quietly confident about this one. I am not on cloud nine yet though, partly because I may be wrong about my chances but also because when I phoned Amy to tell her about the interview, she was a bit distant, a bit non-committal with me. She has been a bit less warm with me since the encounters she had with my ex, first on my doorstep and then on hers. I haven't actually met up with her since then but we have spoken on the phone a few times.

Amy doesn't need the hassle of more family rows and I worry that she is weighing up whether our relationship is worth the trouble. I have been doing some more thinking too. I don't like to give ground to my ex but I have been trying to work out in my head how my relationship with Amy can work in a way that doesn't adversely affect the kids.

If I do spend more time with Amy, and I still very much hope I will, then I reckon I should see her more on the days that I haven't got my children with me. But even then, Lucy spends most of her time with her mum so she will be around. What will Jack think if I am at Amy's? He will probably want to be there too. With school starting soon, it wouldn't be right for Jack to spend his weekday evenings at his girlfriend's.

Whole family sleepovers just seem totally impractical. Although Sean doesn't seem to give a monkey's about my relationship with Amy or Jack's liaison with Lucy, he would probably come to resent being at Amy's with me when Jack is spending all his waking hours with Lucy. And then there is the teenage experimentation with sex issue.

And what about when Jack and Lucy split up? Presumably Jack wouldn't want to see Lucy again. He wouldn't want to go to Amy's with me then.

At the moment, all I have are a lot of unresolved issues.

Sunday 24th August

A few of the lads met up for beers in the Raynes Park Tavern last night. There wasn't an occasion to celebrate as such, but it was a Saturday night and the sun was out so it felt like a good idea to have a drink. Us unmarried folk can do that impromptu stuff you know, at least when the kids are with our ex-other halves.

I had invited Amy along too but I wasn't optimistic that she would come in view of recent events.

I got to the pub slightly later than planned because, not having much to do all day, I fell asleep in front of the telly (god, I am turning into my parents) and didn't wake up until the pints had started flowing. So when I walked in to the pub I was slightly surprised to see Ray (the 'hot' one) in earnest conversation with my Amy. Notice I am getting possessive all of a sudden. The others were propping up the bar. I sidled up to Ray and asked if he had brought his new woman with him.

'Evening Graham. Meet Amy, my brother's wife,' Ray replied. Shit, that was who Amy's ex had reminded me of. Ray.

'Ex-wife,' corrected Amy hurriedly as she gave me a kiss.

Ex-wife is bad enough. More tangled webs. There are quite a few fish in the sea. Even allowing for the fact that some are too young, some too old, some gay et cetera, I have to pick my mate's brother's ex to fall for. Still, I suppose at least she isn't my mate's ex.

Amy pulled a face that said something like 'well, if my daughter is snogging his son, and if I have to deal with his ex shouting at me, then how much more hassle can it be to have him knowing my ex's brother?' Or it might just have been saying 'for fuck's sake'. I didn't really get the chance to talk properly to Amy all night. We still have to work through the various complications of our relationship. The fact that she bothered to turn up at all tonight was a good sign though.

Ray also looked a bit awkward when he realised I was with his brother's ex. My other drinking mates just thought it was highly amusing. When we told them about Jack and Lucy, we spent a good couple of rounds (time is measured in rounds rather than minutes when you are drinking) working out what family relationship there would be between Ray (Lucy's uncle) and me (Jack's dad) if Lucy and Jack tied the knot.

As the evening progressed, I eventually gave into temptation and cornered Ray.

'Why did they split up then?' I asked.

'I think it had something to do with a Spanish au pair,' replied Ray. 'Or maybe it was because my brother got jealous every time he saw Amy talking to another bloke and ended up putting the guy in hospital.'

I think he was joking about the jealousy thing but I am not sure.

Bryan turned up later in the evening so the conversation quickly moved from my relationships to what Tracey was like in bed (still noisy but now also a bit too dominant for Bryan's liking). There was one slightly awkward moment when Bryan called Amy Julia but I think I got away with it as Amy just thought he was pissed.

Wednesday 27th August

I got the job! The assistant director of something or other phoned me up today and offered it to me. She was impressed with my application and slightly worryingly, she told me my answers to the interview questions show that I can think outside the box.

The next step before they formally offer me the job is that they take references. The woman from Merton asked me how I came to know Richard Branson. 'Oh, I met him whilst saving the tigers,' I told her. I am beginning to wonder whether putting Branson as my referee was such a good idea now.

There is just under a month until my birthday and dare I say it, things are going OK. I am becoming a bit more self-confident, I have a fairly decent social life, I am in a relationship albeit a complicated one, I have a flat and a new job subject to references. My relationship with the kids is good despite Sean's broken heel.

Today I even started giving some thought to my birthday party. I am mulling over two options. I could splash out and hire a local club for a disco. I am not sure I am ready to subject Amy to my dancing skills though, so at the moment I am favouring just hiring the function room at the Morden

Brook and putting on a buffet. Hopefully the karaoke Elvis will be on in the main bar for some added entertainment.

Thursday 28th August

My sister Hills just phoned to tell me that she and Donna are having a baby. Them both being women, I didn't know what to say. I dismissed 'How is that physically possible' as too intrusive; 'Aren't you a bit old for that?' as a bit rude and 'Haven't you had enough already?' as even more rude. In the end I opted for, 'How nice. When's it due?' February apparently.

It has only just occurred to me that I don't know which of them is actually having the baby. Still, I shouldn't concern myself with the details.

Saturday 30th August

Sean hasn't visited my flat since the accident as it would have taken forever for him to have managed the three flights of stairs. But today both boys came round as Sean is getting more nimble on his crutches. His plaster comes off soon – ironically about two days after the last cricket match of the season.

The boys hadn't been here for five minutes when I walked in to the front room to find them reading a scrunched up piece of paper.

'Is that Lucy's mum, dad?' Jack asked, holding out the paper. I took it from him. It was the article Amy was writing when she stayed here a couple of weeks ago. She must have printed it off but forgotten to take it with her in her haste to leave when my ex turned up.

Sex after marriage

Once upon a time I remember loving sex, but then I got married and had a baby. Overnight my husband and I went from sex toys to cuddly toys and from 'raw sex' to 'making love'. We progressed fairly rapidly from 'making love' to 'not tonight dear I've got a headache'. In short, I became a bored housewife. Sex became a birthday treat. We didn't even do it at Christmas because by bedtime alcohol had taken its toll.

But at least I had a husband who didn't abuse me; who was a good dad to our daughter when he eventually got home from work; and who provided for us financially. I was in my comfort zone even if my erogenous zone wasn't seeing much action.

As my regular readers will know, I used to dream about good sex. Let's be honest, I used to dream about any sex. Would I ever rediscover a love of sex again? I used to wonder whether there could be such thing as sex after marriage. I worried about this in the same way that other people ponder the existence of life after death.

One morning when my golf coach cancelled on me, my husband showed me in glorious technicolour that there is such a thing as sex after marriage. I came home to find him and the au pair in flagrante, in the act, in the buff, on my Italian leather sofa. He was enjoying sex after marriage (our marriage officially stopped when I walked in on them) ergo sex after marriage must exist.

That was a year ago. The au pair has long since gone back to Spain leaving my ex on his own (shame) and I have started rebuilding my life.

Without actually drawing up a project plan and going about it with military precision, I have spent some of the last year rediscovering my love for sex. And as it happens, I have achieved my goal. In my last article for this magazine (I am no longer a bored housewife), I want to share the three steps I took with you as you may find them useful in your situation.

Firstly I have started paying attention to my own body again. Many married women take themselves for granted, let themselves go to seed, put on a few pounds here and there or let their personal grooming habits slip slightly. Let's face it, our men let themselves go so why shouldn't we? I know I did when I was married.

I will never turn myself into a 21-year-old au pair with a perfect rear end, but over the past year I have at least aspired to become a MILF. I have put myself back in the shop window rather than in some dark and dingy corner in the back of the grannies' discount cardigans section.

Secondly, practice makes perfect as they say. You won't rediscover a love for sex without actually having sex. I am not ashamed to confess that I have had a few one-night stands. They were all slightly unsatisfactory. The first was a bit of a fumble, the second was over in seconds and the third was very pleasant but I think he liked me - awkward. These one-night stands have served their purpose. After fifteen years of only getting naked in front of one man, I have now overcome my inhibitions and rebuilt my confidence. As a bonus I have also learnt a few new tricks for future use in the bedroom.

And thirdly, within the last month or so I have found a man who I can enjoy sex with. Finding a new man was part of my master plan. You can't buy a new man to order but you can put yourself 'out there', be open to meeting new people. I met him walking my dog of all things.

One dog walk led to another and one thing led to another.

Our dalliances may not be the all-action shagging we get to see so often in raunchy Hollywood blockbusters but we do at least disturb a few cushions. I am now looking forward to that period where we spend hours getting to know each other's bodies, how to please each other in a hundred different ways and in every room in the house. Not to mention the garden. The joy of discovering a new body and of someone else discovering yours is something to behold.

The grass may not always be greener, but sometimes it just is.
Amy
Ex bored housewife.

Well, who'd have thought it? I am not sure what to make of that. I suppose if nothing else it makes me feel better about my indiscretion with Julia. The other thought that occurred to me is did I use a condom?

'What's an au pair?' Sean asked as I finished reading the article.

'Never mind that,' Jack muttered from the armchair, 'I hope you haven't 'pleased each other' in this chair. Gross.'

Once the boys had gone back to their mum's, I texted Amy. We still haven't slipped back in to our stride with each other since the incidents with my ex so I didn't feel relaxed enough to phone her. Our text chat was fairly friendly though.

Me: 'My boys just found your 'sex after marriage' article down the side of my sofa. x'

Amy: 'Shit, sorry. x'

Me: 'Did you mean all that stuff about the one night stands? x'

Amy: 'Sorry again. They meant nothing. x'

Me: 'Never mind. I am just looking forward to having sex in every room in your double-fronted house. You must have a hundred rooms.'

Monday 1ˢᵗ September

Someone from Merton Council contacted me this afternoon and told me they were having problems getting hold
of one of my referees. I told them that, as far as I know,
Richard Branson is out of the country for the foreseeable
future and they might struggle getting hold of him. 'Have
you got his mobile number?' she asked. 'No, but I know he
is with Virgin Mobile if that's any help,' I replied. She said
she'd try directory enquiries.

Wednesday
3rd September

It's official. As of 15th September I am going to be a fully functioning member of society again. Either Richard Branson came through with my reference or Merton gave up on him and relied on my good character. That is excellent news for financial reasons, but also because now that the World Cup and the cricket have finished, I am having to resort to daytime telly.

I was supposed to be hosting round three of our Raynes Park set dinner party tonight. Katie and Bryan, John and Tracey, Julia and I all put the date in our diaries at the end of the last dinner party. But with Katie now an alcoholic, Bryan sleeping with Tracey, not a clue who if anyone John is sleeping with and me having had a one night stand with Julia and now being with Amy, I decided on reflection to cancel the planned dinner.

Instead I phoned Amy and asked her if she fancied coming over. She politely declined, citing some issue with Lucy. Something about her tone made me wonder whether she was being evasive. She sounded a bit reserved. Other than at the pub with the lads that Saturday night, I haven't seen Amy for a fortnight. We haven't been talking as much on the phone either. It just hasn't been the same since my ex met her twice in a couple of days. Amy did at least agree to meet me for a pizza in Wimbledon on Friday but I didn't get the sense that she was looking forward to it.

Until the last week or so, I was beginning to feel more confident about my future. It was to be a future shared with Amy and, at least for part of the time, with my boys. I had felt that I was building a new life, a new normal. But now things are looking decidedly less optimistic. I know what I want. I want Amy. I will make that clear to her on Friday.

Friday 5ᵗʰ September

I didn't get the chance to make my feelings clear.

I got to the restaurant over the road from the theatre slightly early and took the liberty of ordering us both a Peroni. I wasn't sure whether this would end up being a romantic dinner or not. I couldn't help fearing that Amy might turn it in to an intolerable parting of the ways. Other than to confirm she would be at the restaurant at seven, she hasn't been answering my texts in the last couple of days.

I had nearly finished my beer by the time Amy turned up. As soon as I saw her push open the door, I knew she had an agenda for tonight, and not an agenda I would like either. She wasn't her normal smiling, care-free self. She looked tired.

As she sat down I leant forward to give her a kiss. She presented her cheek. That didn't bode well either. 'What's up?' I asked.

'Your wife came to see me yesterday.'

'My ex?'

'Your ex.'

'What did she want?' I asked, already feeling my hackles raising.

'She asked how I would feel if my fourteen-year-old daughter was regularly staying over with her boyfriend.'

'What, she wants Lucy to stay with Jack?' I asked incredulously.

'No, the opposite. She doesn't want you and me sleeping together. It sets a bad example for Jack and Lucy.'

'Why didn't she talk to me about this?' Count to ten Graham, count to ten.

'I told her that. She said you would get pissed at her.'

'Too right I would.' What a bloody cheek. What right did my ex have talking to Amy about our love lives? What right did she have talking to Amy about our children?

'She has got a point though, hasn't she?' Amy observed. My ex might be one hundred per cent right, but I didn't need to hear Amy agreeing with her right now.

'Maybe she has, but it didn't stop you asking me to stay when you knew Lucy was home the other day,' I pointed out.

'Lucy is my daughter. I am responsible for her and I can talk to her.' Amy was frowning. This conversation wasn't easy for her.

'I am responsible for Jack. I can talk to him too,' I argued.

Amy went on to tell me that my ex had also brought up the subject of the impact of his father and brother's relationships on Sean. Eventually she chucked in my ex's punchline. 'Your ex told me she would talk to her solicitor about ending your visitation rights if we continue to set a bad example to Sean.'

And breathe. Who does my ex think she is? Admittedly, mine and Jack's relationships with Amy and Lucy are far from conventional, but they make us happy. I haven't always thought of all of the possible consequences of our complicated situation but I haven't done anything crass or inappropriate. I haven't suggested that the boys and I all sleep at Amy's. I haven't slept with Amy while Jack and Sean have been with me. I haven't left Jack and Lucy alone together in a bedroom. I haven't even left Sean alone with Jack and Amy because I wouldn't want him feeling like a gooseberry. There have been no sordid orgies. My ex needs to chill out.

'Graham, I just don't know that I can deal with the hassle of having your ex looking over my shoulder right now,' Amy concluded. 'I have just about got my own ex out of my life. The last thing I need is someone else's throwing their weight around.'

I was a little bit shell-shocked. Not to mention a little bit angry. I sat there nursing my empty beer bottle, not trusting myself to say anything. After what seemed like ages but was probably only a minute or so, the waitress approached to take our order. Amy pushed her chair back and walked out of the restaurant with a tear running down her cheek. Was she walking out of my life too?

That all happened a couple of hours ago. I hung around at the restaurant for a while after Amy had gone in case she changed her mind and came back. She didn't. Since I got home, I have been gazing in to the bottom of a bottle of lager reflecting upon events. The more I think about it, the more I think my ex is totally out of order. I haven't been a bad role model or exposed my children to anything inappropriate. For a while tonight I contemplated going straight round to my ex's and ranting at her. In the end I didn't bother. She isn't the important one right now. She can prattle on with her empty threats all she likes but I am not going to dignify them with a response.

What tonight has made me realise is how much I want to be with Amy. When I am not with her I miss her laughter, I miss her scent. I miss her touch. Amy has got to be my priority, not ranting at my ex. Where would ranting at my ex get me anyway? Amy didn't categorically say she doesn't want to see me anymore, but she didn't say she does want to see me either. I am not sure where we stand. Are we still an item?

Starting from tomorrow I am going to do my best to make sure we are.

Saturday 6th September

I don't know how to say this other than to just come out with it. Amy is in a coma in St George's Hospital. She went to pick Lucy up from her ex's after she left me at the restaurant last night but she didn't get there. She was knocked down.

I didn't find out until this morning. Jack phoned me first. And then Ray phoned. I don't know any details yet. All Ray could tell me is that his brother and Amy's mother are at the hospital by Amy's bedside.

I can't believe it. I feel totally lost, dazed, overwhelmed. I have never experienced trauma like this before. No one I have been close to has ever ended up in intensive care. Grandparents have died but that is meant to happen. Amy is my age. She isn't meant to die.

She can't die. I didn't even say goodbye to her when she left the restaurant. She doesn't know how I feel about her. Why didn't I tell her yesterday when I had the chance? We haven't even done a fraction of the things that couples do together. We haven't stayed in on a wet night and watched a film. We haven't welcomed each other home from work with a kiss and a steaming hot plate of food. We haven't argued about where to go on holiday. We haven't argued. She can't die without us having had a good dingdong. She can't die because the last time I saw her, she had a tear in her eye.

I am being selfish. She can't die because she has Lucy to mother. Jack had heard the news from Amy's distraught daughter. He wants to come over to the flat but I put him off because I want to go to the hospital. I want to be there for Amy, to hold her hand, to tell her we will get through this together, to tell her it will be alright. Ray tried to put me off going to the hospital. I am not interested in having a scene with his brother but I am not going to stay away from Amy either. I told Ray I would go this afternoon and if his brother was still there, he would just have to deal with me turning up.

I have spent the last couple of hours trying to function, to do things, anything that will stop me going straight to the hospital. I just washed up my breakfast stuff. I could see cars passing on the road below my window. Dogs were barking too. All around my flat, life is carrying on. The traffic lights are still changing colour. Leaves on the trees are still shifting in the breeze. But, to me, today the world is on hold. Everything has stopped except for Amy's struggle for life. Nothing else matters.

I am off to the hospital.

Sunday 7th September

Amy is in intensive care, still fighting. Luckily the accident happened just down the road from St George's hospital. She hit her head pretty hard. The surgeons operated on her almost straight away on Friday night to relieve the pressure on her swollen brain. She has been kept in an induced coma since the accident to give her brain time to recover. This afternoon we were told that the treatment seems to be working as the swelling is going down. They are going to reduce her medication over the next day or so and hopefully bring her out of her coma. No one official is making any predictions yet, though, about her long-term health.

When I arrived at the hospital yesterday and eventually found the right wing, the right floor and the right section, I immediately recognised Amy's mother sitting in a waiting area next to a nurse's station. Amy has her mother's hair and her mother's eyes.

'Hi, you must be Imogen. I'm Graham,' I said, holding out my alcohol-rubbed hand.

'Graham,' she repeated in a tired voice while nodding to herself. She showed no recognition of my name. No interest in me either. She just continued to stare at one of a number of curtained-off areas across the room. My hand was left dangling un-grasped until I awkwardly withdrew it.

You are supposed to meet parents of partners over dinner, or drinks, or if you are really lucky you wouldn't need to meet them at all. You certainly aren't supposed to meet them in a hospital waiting area with busy health professionals moving purposefully to and fro around you. You aren't supposed to meet them when the person you have in common is fighting for her life.

I sat down opposite Imogen and waited. Isn't that what you do in waiting areas? I hadn't heard anything about Amy's condition at that point other than what Ray had told me on the phone. I didn't want to intrude on Imogen's thoughts but I had to know. I asked her how Amy was. Finally she seemed to register that there was someone else present.

'What did you say your name was again?' she asked.

'Graham. Graham Hope. I'm Amy's, er, I am a friend of Amy's,' I managed.

Imogen nodded again and then proceeded to tell me in hushed tones about the operation to relieve the pressure on Amy's brain. When she had finished, I asked if I could see Amy.

'There's someone in with her at the moment,' Imogen replied. And at that moment Ray's brother, also known as Amy's ex, also known as Stuart, brushed aside the curtain that Imogen had been studying so intently and walked over to us.

Imogen stood up. 'Has anything changed?' she asked anxiously. Stuart shook his head. And then he focussed on me.

'Who are you?'

'Hi, you must be Stuart. I'm Graham,' I said, holding out my hand and having the proffered handshake refused for the second time in ten minutes. Did I overdo it on the alcohol rub?

'Ray has told me about you. I don't give a shit if you are his mate. As far as I am concerned you can piss off.' A young nurse lifted her head up from the paperwork she was studying and gave us both a withering look. She was about to say something when Imogen stepped in and put a stop to our unseemly banter.

I didn't get in to see Amy yesterday. As Stuart pointed out in no uncertain terms, I am not family. Technically speaking, now that he is divorced from Amy, neither is he. But in fear of getting a smack I decided not to push the point.

When I went back to the hospital today, Stuart wasn't there. The curtains around Amy's bed were closed, as were those around the other patients. It struck me how quiet it was in the intensive care unit. Other than the hum of mechanical noise from the machines keeping the people on this ward alive, there was little noise at all from the patients. Presumably they were all sedated like Amy.

I was pleading my case with the same nurse who had given us the look yesterday to let me go in and see Amy when Imogen stuck her head around the curtain and beckoned me in.

I have watched my fair share of hospital dramas but nothing prepared me for how fragile Amy looked. Her head from her eyes upwards was pretty much covered in bandages. Wires and tubes were feeding in to space-aged machines at the side of her bed. The machines were beeping and gurgling and displays were flashing, some at regular intervals, some irregularly. I couldn't help wondering if the irregular beeps should have been regular.

Until that point, this whole episode had felt a bit unreal. I was almost going through the motions of saying and doing the right thing. But seeing Amy looking so battered and helpless threw me over the edge. I haven't broken down so completely since, well, ever. Imogen sat me down in the one bedside chair and kneaded my shoulder while I held my head in my hands.

Amy looked so damaged. The whole left side of her face was scratched raw, presumably from when she landed on the tarmac. Her skin, where it wasn't cut up, looked impossibly pale. It took me a while to compose myself.

Imogen and I sat with Amy for a good hour, both of us mainly lost in our own thoughts about the woman we cared for. Imogen did break her reverie to tell me the news about the doctors gradually reducing her medication in the hope that she would slowly wake from her induced coma. She also told me about Amy's left eye. Something pierced it in the accident. The doctors are concentrating on Amy's brain at the moment but one of them told Imogen this morning that if she does recover, they aren't sure that they will be able to save her eye.

I sat and stroked Amy's fingers. Even her right hand was bandaged, presumably from when she put it out to break her fall. The news about her eye is awful but if her brain doesn't recover sufficiently for her to breathe for herself, then whatever other damage there is will be irrelevant.

After a while we heard Stuart and Lucy arrive on to the ward. Imogen and I withdrew from Amy's cubicle and went down the two flights of stairs and outside for a bit of fresh air, leaving Stuart and Lucy to sit with Amy. And that's where the questioning started.

'How long have you known Amy for?' her mum opened with. I gave her a potted history of Amy and me, mentioning things like the dog walking and our trip to the Lake District but leaving out any mention of Jack and any encounters with my ex. When Imogen asked me if I had met Lucy much before today, I just played a straight bat and said yes.

'I am going to stay at Amy's for a few days so that Lucy can come home,' Imogen announced. 'I can't bear the thought of her staying with that man, even if he is her dad.' So there is no love lost between Imogen and Amy's ex then. I expect the affair with the au pair now shapes Imogen's opinion of him.

Eventually, after exchanging phone numbers with Imogen, I left her at the hospital entrance waiting for Lucy to emerge with her dad. I had no desire to have another face-off with Amy's ex, particularly in front of Lucy.

When I got home I listened to my phone messages. I had several missed calls from my ex's number. I wasn't sure whether it was her or Jack phoning. I dialled the number and my ex picked up.

'I am sorry to hear about what has happened, Graham,' she said.

In view of her previous intervention in mine and Amy's love life, I suspected she was anything but sorry but I didn't have the energy for a confrontation. I asked her to put Jack on.

'How is Lucy's mum, dad?' my boy asked once he had been handed the phone. I filled him in on the latest developments. He had probably heard them all already from Lucy but he wanted to check in case things had moved on.

'Lucy wants me to come to the hospital with her tomorrow,' Jack informed me.

'But it's a school day tomorrow son,' I rather stuffily told him.

'Mum says that if it is OK with you then I can come,' he pleaded.

I agreed to think about it. If I take Jack along tomorrow then Imogen will get to see the full me/Amy, Jack/Lucy picture, but then why shouldn't she see it? I phoned her once I had got off the phone with Jack and arranged to drive Lucy to the hospital in the morning. I didn't mention Jack though. I offered Imogen a lift too but she said she would make her own way there a bit earlier than the 9 o'clock I was suggesting.

It has been a long weekend. I am mentally and physically

exhausted. I hardly slept last night. Tonight I have had a couple of fingers of Scotch to help me relax. I don't think I have eaten anything all day so the whisky has gone straight to my head.

I put the telly on to take the edge off the silence in the flat. The first image I saw was a photo of Amy. As well as describing Amy's condition as 'critical but stable', the local news was appealing for witnesses to the accident. The car driver hadn't stopped at the scene.

When you gossip about someone being injured, you immediately talk about how it happened. But when that someone happens to be someone close to you, all that matters is that they get better. Until now I hadn't even given a thought to how the accident had happened. Now though, as well as being wracked with panic over the possibility of losing Amy, I have found a bit of room in my heart to hate the bastard who, to all intents and purposes, left Amy for dead on Garratt Lane.

I have said before that shit happens to those that let shit happen. It also obviously happens to those that don't. Basically, shit happens. I shouldn't mess with a well-established phrase.

Monday 8th September

Jack and I picked Lucy up from her Wimbledon Village home and took her to see her mum. It was heartwarming seeing Jack sitting in the back of the car holding hands with Lucy, being there for her in her time of need. How my eldest son has grown up over the last few months. I wish he hadn't had to grow up so fast but now that he has, he is doing an excellent job of it.

My boy has been doing his research on brain injuries too. He reminded Lucy about Jesse Ryder, the New Zealand cricketer who made a full recovery from a coma. I notice he didn't mention Michael Schumacher though.

Imogen was at the hospital when we arrived. I introduced Jack.

'I have heard all about you from Lucy,' Imogen said to Jack, 'and I am pleased to finally meet you, young man.'

Turning to me, 'But I didn't know Jack and you knew each other?'

'I have known him since he was born,' I told her. Imogen smiled and we left it at that.

The doctors were in with Amy when we arrived. To give them a chance to give us the full picture without having to worry about sweetening the pill for the sake of the children, I sent the two young love birds off with some money to get themselves a snack. The hospital staff wouldn't have allowed the four of us in to see Amy at the same time anyway.

Eventually the two doctors emerged from Amy's cubicle, notes in hand. As soon as I saw them emerge, I started looking for any tell-tale early signs as to whether the news was good or not. The younger of the two was smiling and nodding away at his older colleague's words. The older one, who subsequently introduced himself as Mr Crane, wasn't smiling but he didn't look unduly pensive or concerned either. Mr Crane shook my hand but mainly addressed his update to Imogen because he didn't know how I fit in to the plot.

'Your daughter is still seriously ill but we do think there is some reason to be optimistic,' he informed us, to our immense relief. 'This morning's scans have shown us that the swelling on her brain has continued to decrease. We are really pleased with the progress she is making. We will have a much better idea about her prospects by tomorrow. In fact, the next few days are critical.'

You don't exactly have to be a brain surgeon to see that.

Mr Crane also reminded us how lucky we were that the accident had happened so close to the hospital. And not just any hospital but St George's in particular. "This hospital is a major trauma hospital and has an excellent neurology department. We had the staff and equipment to operate straight away. If your daughter's accident had happened anywhere else, we might be having a very different conversation right now."

Mr Crane's words left me feeling cold. It's hard to think that someone is lucky when they get run over but in this case, it seems that Amy certainly was. I don't want to imagine what would have happened if she had been run over somewhere else.

I stayed at the hospital for the morning. I had told Jack on the way over to picking Lucy up that he may not get in to see Amy, but that if he did, he should be prepared for what he would see. In the end, Lucy went in with her grandmother. Jack and I waited outside.

'What if she's brain damaged?' Jack asked me when we were on our own.

If truth be told, I haven't got a clue what will happen if Amy doesn't recover fully. She lives on her own with Lucy. If she comes through the accident but with a loss of some of her mental or physical faculties then who would help look after both of them? From what I know of Amy, she would hate to rely on her ex for anything. How much would her mum help? How much could I help?

I don't even know the answer to that last question. I have just got myself a full-time job. Practically, how much could I do? I know I am sounding a bit of a sap but I have fallen for Amy big time. She has put the colour back into my life over the last couple of months. When I am with her I am no longer a divorced man but a man with a life. She makes me smile. She is the first person I want to share life's events with.

But is all that enough? What if she doesn't regain all her faculties? What if she isn't the woman I fell in love with? They do talk about people who have suffered a brain injury changing their personality, becoming more snappy and moody. I couldn't cope if Amy turned into my ex all over again.

All I could think of to say to Jack was, 'Let's hope we don't have to cross that bridge, son.'

Much to Jack's annoyance, I dropped him off at school at lunchtime. I then nipped round to see if my ex was in. She was. I needed to talk to her about the whole relationship thing. Adult to adult. I don't yet know whether or not Amy will make a full recovery. I am trying not to dwell on the negative thoughts though. When she does come out of hospital, fighting fit and ready to resume her life, I want our relationship to go back to how it was before my ex stuck the boot in. Which was why I found myself sitting in my old kitchen having coffee with my ex this lunchtime.

'You look as though you haven't slept in days,' she observed once she had invited me in.

I didn't really know where to start. I didn't have the mental capacity to plan the conversation out in my head so I just jumped right in.

'Has Jack talked to you about Lucy?'

'Yes, all the time,' my ex admitted. 'He tells me she is his soul mate and that if I try and get in the way of him seeing her, he will move in with you.'

I was too tired to smile at that. Even if I wasn't too tired I am not sure I would have smiled. We can't have the kids playing one of us off against the other. I still believe in presenting a united front to the kids when possible.

I did my best to convince my ex that I was an appropriate adult, acting appropriately. 'I know it must be hard for you because you aren't as involved as me in that part of his life, but I do supervise what they are up to. They still operate within ground rules.'

'I know,' she acknowledged, 'it is just that he is growing up. He's having new adventures and I am not involved in them.' Welcome to my world.

She went on to ask me whether I had talked to Jack about sex.

'I have talked to him about kissing, but as far as I can tell he was embarrassed enough about that. There is no way he is going to be getting his willy out any time soon.' That seemed to pacify her.

We then talked about Sean and the effect that the father and son, mother and daughter thing might have on him. Sean has never said a bad word about what is going on. He seems to like Amy. That, above everything else, is probably the hardest part for my ex to deal with. She did though seem genuinely sorry that she had threatened to get her solicitor involved if I carried on seeing Amy. 'I was at a low point,' she confessed. 'Mark and I had split up. You were getting your life back together, Jack was growing up. It just felt like it was me and Sean against the world. I lashed out at you. I'm sorry.'

My ex is very into rotas, lists and ground rules. She has rules for everything, from who is washing up each night right through to a behaviour code that the children must abide by. By the time I had drunk my latte and headed back to the hospital, I had agreed a set of four simple ground rules with my ex that would govern mine and Jack's relationships with Amy and Lucy. I undertook:

1. Not to sleep over at Amy's when I am looking after Jack and Sean.

2. Not to let Amy and Lucy sleep over at my flat when Jack and Sean are there. This rule is unnecessary because my flat isn't big enough to accommodate a mass sleep-over. I didn't bother pointing that out to my ex though.

3. Not to let Jack spend extended periods of time alone with Lucy upstairs. This one will be harder to enforce because he goes to Lucy's without me being there sometimes.

4. Not to let Sean ever feel like the odd one out.

I was quite happy to agree to abide by these rules if it meant that my ex got off my back. I had pretty much come to these conclusions on my own anyway.

I felt slightly happier as I drove back to the hospital. Now all that remains in the way of mine and Amy's relationship is Amy's recovery and her acceptance of my baggage.

Tuesday 9th September

The long road to recovery has started. Imogen phoned me first thing this morning and gave me the good news. I rushed straight over to the hospital. I got to the intensive care ward and received the shock of my life when I saw an empty space where Amy's bed had been. A nurse soon put me straight, telling me she had been moved out of the intensive care ward and into a high dependency neurology ward upstairs. I guess Amy not being in intensive care now must be a good sign.

When I found the right ward, I joined Imogen in another sterile waiting area.

There are no miracles in life. Amy didn't smile at me, sit up and give me a hug as soon as I walked in to her room. But she did blink a few times with her right eye. Her left eye is still swollen and covered. Holding her hand felt different. It sounds stupid but it felt like she was more 'there' than she was yesterday. Her fingers moved, not to the extent that they gripped mine or anything, but I could feel movement.

As the day wore on, blinks graduated to attempts at smiles. Finger movement moved on to positive gripping and Amy began to move her head, albeit painfully and slowly. She definitely recognised us all. The initial signs are that she hasn't suffered any catastrophic brain damage.

I was about to leave the hospital for the day, feeling tired but slightly more chipper now that Amy is noticeably on the mend, when a nurse told me there were two police officers in the hospital's main reception area waiting to talk to Imogen and me. On the way down to find them, we speculated that they had come to give us news of who had knocked Amy down. It turned out, though, that they wanted to discover information rather than impart it.

The two officers, a Sergeant Atkinson and his sidekick PC Reynolds, wanted to talk to me first. I sat with them answering their questions for about ten minutes. They were pleasant and genial with me but it all felt a bit odd. Until that point I had assumed that some idiot had run Amy down through a simple lack of attention to their driving. From the nature of their questions though, it sounded as though the police had other ideas. At one point, they asked me where I was at the time of the accident.

'Look, what the bloody hell is going on here?' I asked. 'I thought Amy was knocked down by some drunk who failed to stop.'

'She probably was,' Sgt. Atkinson agreed, 'but we wouldn't be doing our jobs properly if we didn't look in to all the options, would we?'

So I told them about that Friday night, how Amy and I had met up in Wimbledon but subsequently gone our separate ways, my way being to the 164 bus stop and back to my flat.

'Did you have an argument that night?' the PC asked.

'No.' Strictly speaking, I wouldn't classify our discussion as an argument.

'Do you know whether Amy had any enemies?' I felt like I was in the middle of a Mark Billingham novel and that any minute, Tom Thorne would grab me by the lapels (not that I had a jacket on) and try and shake a confession out of me.

'I don't know her friends, let alone her enemies,' I replied. I can't imagine that Amy would have any enemies. Who would want to run her down? That sort of thing just doesn't happen to ordinary people, does it?

Sitting back at my flat having the regulation Scotch before bed, I am totally relieved that Amy isn't going to die on us. I won't relax though until I have heard her speak, until I have heard her laugh.

As well as worrying about Amy's health, I have now started thinking about the hit and run. No matter how much I think about it, I can't believe that this can be anything other than a tragic accident. I guess the police are right to pursue all options but on this occasion they must be barking up the wrong tree. Imogen agreed. Her verdict was that the police were just covering their arses.

Thursday 11th September

Amy is now able to talk. She was slurring her words a bit yesterday but even that has cleared up today. She is up and about but she is still unsteady, wobbly on her feet. She is still a bit confused too. She doesn't remember anything from around the time she passed out. I have exhibited a few of these symptoms after a good night out.

The first thing she said to me when I got to the hospital yesterday afternoon was, 'You need a shave.' I was impressed that she could see that much, what with one eye bandaged up and the other like an island in the centre of bruised flesh. Maybe she felt my stubble when I kissed her.

She hasn't got her head around her eyesight issue yet. The doctors haven't totally written off her left eye but their brows furrow whenever they look under the bandage. An eye specialist is coming to see her tomorrow.

Rather than her eye issue, Amy seems totally preoccupied with the amount of scarring she will be left with once the bruising subsides and the remaining bandages are removed. The first question she asks any medical professional who comes in to see her is, 'How are my cuts healing up?'

I am not proud of myself but her cuts and scarring concern me too. I know the arguments. Beauty is only skin deep, it's the person inside that matters. That's easy to say but it's much harder to feel. The left side of her face is still one giant black, brown and green bruise with big welts of scratched skin running from under her ear, across her cheek to her nose. I can't help worrying that Amy won't ever fully recover her former unblemished skin, gorgeous eyes and smile.

Imogen saw me looking at Amy. A bit later when I went to grab a sandwich from the hospital canteen, she asked if she could join me. I have spent countless hours with Amy's mother over the past few days. We have got on well enough but our focus hasn't been on each other. I haven't discovered much about Imogen and she doesn't know much about me. Imogen had obviously decided that it was high time we put an end to that state of affairs.

'What are your intentions, Graham?' she asked, just as I was taking my first bite out of my cheese and cucumber sandwich in the noisy canteen. It struck me as quite an old fashioned question, quite formal. But also quite pertinent.

What are my intentions? I do want a long term future with Amy. In my mind at least, our relationship has already exceeded the 'casual' tag because of the extent of my feelings for Amy. I am not saying I necessarily want to marry her. I am not sure I will ever be the marrying type again. But I catch myself thinking of a future in which Amy and I are growing old together, dine at posh restaurants, take trips to the theatre and receive regular house-calls from our adult children, possibly with their own children in tow. I haven't got anywhere near discussing any of this with Amy. I am really not sure if she feels the same, but I am certainly hoping she does.

I shared these thoughts with Imogen. She smiled but needed more convincing. 'I saw the way you were looking at her earlier. I know what you must be thinking. Amy isn't looking her best at the moment and she is probably not going to regain the sight in her eye. Are you really going to stand by her? Are you going to be there for her when she's looking in the mirror and sobbing? Are you going to help her with Lucy? Are you going to help her through the nightmares about the accident? What I am asking you, Graham, is do you love my daughter as much as I do?'

I hesitated before answering. It isn't that I am worried about commitment. I'm not. It isn't that I don't love Amy. I do. Do I? I do. Yes, I do. I love Amy. I am in love with her. I am, though, still trying to get my head around the looks thing and any other long-term damage that Amy might have suffered. My ex would tell you that I am a rubbish nursemaid. And to be fair, on this point she would be right. She always took on that role in our marital home.

Imogen seized upon my hesitation. 'If you aren't sure, Graham, then just leave us in peace. Go now. Let me support my daughter. She has been hurt before by Stuart, she is physically hurting now and I don't want her to have to go through anything else that upsets her.'

Amy's mum sat there, staring intently at me, almost challenging me to get up and walk out of her daughter's life. I didn't go. I remained firmly planted to my seat and ate the rest of my sandwich in silence.

Imogen and I continued to interact as the afternoon wore on. She isn't giving me the cold shoulder or anything like that but she is quite a formidable woman. She knows I am wrestling with my emotions. She has made it clear that she doesn't want any half-arsed commitment. She wants me to either get with the programme or get lost.

I need to sort my head out.

Friday 12th September

Exactly a week after the accident, the doctors have confirmed that Amy will never be able to see out of her left eye again. They spelt out all the technical details but we couldn't take them in. They have told us that all they can do is perform cosmetic surgery that will reduce the visual impact of Amy's injuries to her eye and eye socket. In other words they can improve what her eye looks like but not what it looks at.

Over the last day or two, Amy has begun to grasp the significance of this news. This afternoon, after the doctors had left us to ourselves, she reeled off a list of things she wouldn't be able to do again. Uppermost on Amy's mind was driving, followed closely by skiing. She seems such a capable person. The thought of not being able to do things, of being clumsy and needing help, terrifies her. Imogen told me she had never seen Amy so down before.

I took Jack and Sean out for a pizza this evening. I haven't seen much of Sean lately. He is having his plaster removed on Monday. I gave them both an update on Amy's condition. When I told them about Amy's eye, Sean put his hand over his left eye and looked around.

'You can still see everything with one eye, dad. You just have to look a bit harder.' I hadn't really thought of it like that. It isn't as though Amy will only be able to see half as much now as she could before the accident. Still, it will take some getting used to.

It has been a long week.

Sunday 14th September

Now I know that Amy will be around on this earth for some time to come, normal life is gradually beginning to force its way back in to my consciousness again. I have stopped resenting the traffic lights changing colour. I no longer mind everyone else carrying on their business as usual. As a case in point, I went clothes shopping today. My new job starts tomorrow. It wouldn't make a good first impression if I turned up for my first day in my slightly shiny-kneed, dog-hair-impregnated trousers and my faded-under-the-arms shirts.

Going back to work will be a challenge. It will be hard for me to concentrate on anything other than Amy. After a couple of months spent not working, the early mornings will also be a shock to the system. So will the need to actually do some work when I am there. On the positive side, assuming the job can hold my interest for longer than five minutes, it will be another goal ticked off my list.

Talking of my list, it is my birthday in just under two weeks' time. When I went to visit Amy this afternoon, she came up with an off the wall idea for a party. Apparently Lucy's birthday is three days before mine. Although I didn't know any of this until today, the intention had been for Lucy to have a few friends to stay on Friday night for a disco at their house. Amy obviously doesn't want that to happen while she is in hospital, so she has suggested that Lucy postpones her party for a week. When I pointed out that this would mean Lucy's party would clash with mine, Amy suggested that we have a joint party, or maybe adults in one room with 1980s music and kids in another with modern noise.

Now call me boring and unimaginative but this idea doesn't fill me with joy. When Amy went off to do some physio I jotted down a list of things wrong with her suggestion:

1. Mixing Dave, Ray, Bryan and even Hills and Donna with teenage girls probably isn't the best idea.
2. There will be alcohol at the party.
3. Amy's immaculate house will get trashed – by my mates as much as the children.
4. There is a distinct possibility that Amy will still be in hospital on my birthday. What will happen to the party then?
5. What will happen if Amy and I split up over the next week or so? I still haven't managed to have a conversation with her about the future.
6. What fifteen-year-old would want a bunch of uncool, mostly lecherous adults at their party?
7. There will be bad language flying around. The children might get embarrassed.
8. It's just a bloody stupid idea, OK?

When Amy got back from shuffling up and down the corridor with her physio, she asked me what I thought of the idea.

'Let's do it,' I replied, not having the backbone to say no. At least a joint party ties me to Amy for at least another fortnight.

Monday 15th September

I am now a contributing member of society again. My first day in my new job has passed with not too much drama. I didn't realise how nervous being the new boy in town would make me feel. I was pretty lonely as I walked into a building I didn't know, filled with people I didn't know, talking a language I didn't know.

Apparently it is my job to make sure that my council does better than other councils. I have to monitor and improve things like GCSE results, the percentage of fat children and teenage pregnancy levels. When I say I have to improve teenage pregnancy levels, that means I have to reduce them, not increase them. Note to self: make the kids study harder, feed them more salad and hand out condoms at this joint birthday party. Everyone has to do their bit.

I have already started writing a 'to do list' in my new job:

1. Learn how to use the coffee machine
2. Memorise at least five people's names each day
3. Learn at least five new three-letter acronyms each day. FFS.
4. Google the difference between a 'councillor' and an 'officer'
5. Ask the man sitting opposite me why he bashes the

keyboard so hard when he types. He must be really angry.

6.   And while I am at it, ask him why he insists on wearing those ridiculous-looking braces.

After work I made the daily trek to the hospital. Although Amy is getting headaches and is still dizzy when moving around, the doctors continue to be pleased with her recovery.

I had intended to talk to her tonight about our future. The conversation we had at the pizza place in Wimbledon before her accident seems like a lifetime ago now. I am aching to know where I stand.

As I walked on to the ward, she was sitting on her bed with her head in her hands.

'Hello gorgeous,' I said by way of greeting. Amy looked up. She had been crying.

'I have just looked in the mirror. Don't give me that crap about being gorgeous. I'm a bloody one-eyed mess covered in scratches and bruises,' she responded angrily.

'At least you can see out of one eye then,' I said, trying to be funny. And failing. Spectacularly. Sometimes my mouth works ahead of my brain. I say things that no sane, considered, reasonable, decent, respectful, civil person would say. As soon as the words had spilled out of my mouth I felt crestfallen. I wanted to grab them and pull them back from mid-air and shove them back down my throat. I wanted to press rewind, back out of Amy's room, walk back in again and start over. But it was too late.

'You're fucking hilarious aren't you Graham. It is alright for you. You aren't the one that got thrown over the bonnet of a car going at thirty miles an hour and landed on your head. You aren't the one that has to live with one eye. You aren't the one who just walked straight in to a hospital trolley on the way to the toilet because it was on my left hand side and I didn't even see it. You aren't the one that looks like something out of a fucking horror movie.' By the end of her outburst the tears were flowing again.

I sat on the edge of her bed and tried to give her a hug. She pushed me away.

'I think you had better go,' Imogen said from behind me.

After my performance tonight, I have a better idea where I stand with Amy. Out in the cold.

I need a beer. Dave's mum is not good so he couldn't join me. Ray didn't let me down though. I am meeting him in the Morden Brook at 8 o'clock. It could be a long night.

Tuesday 16th September

The best thing about my new job is that I can walk to work in five minutes. No more crowded, germ-infested Northern line trips for me. The five minute journey was particularly good news today because my hangover made getting up early this morning a physical impossibility.

Ray and I weren't exactly a barrel of laughs in the pub last night. Firstly we raised a glass to Dave's mum, Mrs F, who is slowly losing her battle with cancer. We then moved on to dissect my ongoing woes. I filled Ray in on Amy's condition. He had heard some of it from his brother. Stuart hasn't been at the hospital for the last few days though so Ray wouldn't have heard it all. When I mentioned Stuart's absence to Ray, he confessed that 'the dragon', presumably meaning Imogen, had warned him off. I had guessed as much.

'I saw Stu yesterday,' Ray admitted. 'He is beating himself up about the accident.'

'Why's he beating himself up about it? What's it got to do with him?'

'Amy was feeling ill and asked him if he would drop Lucy off at her house on that Friday night. Stu said no because he was watching some film on the telly. Amy ended up getting her brains smashed in.'

Stuart blames himself for causing the accident. Well, if it is any consolation to him, he isn't alone. I now blame him too.

Ray went on to tell me that his brother had asked him about me. I am not surprised. I had wanted to know about my ex's partner when I had thought he would be spending time with my children. 'What did you tell him?' I asked.

'Not a lot,' Ray said, 'only that you are a paedophile, money-grabbing git who is prone to a bit of domestic violence from time to time.'

'You're an arse.'

'Don't worry, he was more concerned when I told him you were a Chelsea fan.'

I told Ray that his brother probably needn't worry about me anyway because I was doing a pretty good job of ballsing up my relationship with Amy without any interference from him. When Ray asked how, I repeated my crass line to Amy about her at least being able to see how bad she looks.

'You complete twat,' Ray observed. 'That sort of comment is going to take one hell of a bunch of flowers to put right.'

Wednesday
17th September

The police are still looking for the driver who ran Amy down. I know this because my ex phoned me at work. 'I have just been questioned about your woman's accident,' she told me as an opening line. She wasn't happy, and I couldn't say I blamed her. It seems as though they are still pursuing the theory that whoever knocked Amy flying did it deliberately. They asked her similar questions to those they had asked me. But with my ex they delved deeper in to her possible motives for wanting to run Amy down.

'They asked me why we split up. They asked what I thought of your relationship with Amy. They even knew about Jack and his girlfriend. For fuck's sake Graham, I don't need this right now,' my ex told me.

I could have said something along the lines of 'What, they think you tried to kill my girlfriend?' or 'They think you ran over your son's girlfriend's mother?' but I was in an open plan office surrounded by new work colleagues so I opted to stay silent.

Eventually my ex ran out of steam and hung up on me. I hadn't ever contemplated the possibility of the police wanting to talk to my ex about the hit and run. I suppose on paper she might make a good candidate to talk to. Someone on the outside might think she has got a motive. But I know my ex. She might be ever so slightly unhinged from time to time but she wouldn't do something like this. She doesn't care enough about me to be that jealous of Amy. Even if she did, she wouldn't put her life as the mother of our children at risk by doing something so stupid.

Over my medicinal last Scotch of the evening I caught myself wondering what Amy would think if she knew my ex was being interviewed by the police. When I met her on the night of her accident she was complaining about my ex's interference in our lives. This news could be the final nail in the coffin of our relationship.

Thursday 18th September

Until tonight I hadn't seen Amy since Monday night. I haven't been for the last couple of days because I wasn't sure I would be welcome. I wasn't sure I would be welcome today either but I couldn't stand not seeing her. I phoned Amy's mother to see what she recommended I do. Amy is having her broken eye removed tomorrow and, naturally, she is really down in the dumps about her looks. She doesn't want anyone to see her. Imogen advised me not to visit. After thinking long and hard about it, I ignored Imogen's advice and went anyway. I wish I could learn to listen.

Ray would be pleased to know that the bunch of flowers I took with me was the biggest I could carry.

I got to the hospital just as Amy was eating her evening meal. Although she still wore a patch over her left eye, she looked stunning. There may well still be some permanent scarring but her bruising and scratches have faded a lot in the last couple of days.

But it was her hair that nearly took my breath away. To be frank, it had looked a total mess after the accident. The surgeons had cut large chunks of her beautiful auburn locks away to allow the emergency brain surgery to be undertaken without impediment. Since the last time I saw her, someone has managed to cut and restyle it. It's a lot shorter now. I think they call it a pixie cut. No one who looked at Amy's hair now would have an inkling of the state it was in a week ago.

With her left eye out of action, Amy didn't notice me standing in the doorway. She was struggling to eat her dinner. She couldn't get her peas on to her fork and then in to her mouth. I guess your co-ordination is affected if you lose an eye.

I was a bit embarrassed. I thought about backing out quickly and quietly and coming back when she had finished but I didn't act quickly enough. Just as I was creeping out of the door, Amy noticed me.

'Graham, I told mum to tell you not to come,' she said. Hello Graham, nice to see you.

'Your mum did tell me but I ignored her,' I said. 'I miss you.'

Amy dropped her knife and fork and banged her plate down on to her tray. She was miserable and nothing I did seemed to help. In fact everything I did seemed to have the opposite effect. We ended up having one of those big discussions that can shape a relationship. One where the participants get carried away and say things they hadn't intended to say.

'What can I do to help you?' I asked. I went to pick up her fork.

'Oh for god's sake Graham, I don't need you feeding me. I am not a useless toddler, you know.'

'I didn't say you were. I just want to be there for you.' I put the fork back on the tray and placed the tray on the end of the bed out of the way.

'The last thing I want is you fussing over me but secretly feeling sorry for yourself. I don't need a nurse.'

'I'm a crap nurse anyway. I want to be your lover.'

'Oh Graham, I am having my eye removed tomorrow.

I can't look beyond my operation. Can't we do this some other time?'

Amy's ophthalmologist walked in at that point. His timing couldn't have been better because had he not chosen that moment to enter, I was about to point out the irony in Amy's previous words. He saved me from myself. He came to talk her through what they planned to do in tomorrow's operation. Like me, he didn't get off to a very good start.

'It's a fairly routine procedure. I have done quite a few of these over the years,' he announced.

'It may be routine to you but having my eye removed isn't routine to me,' Amy chastised him.

The doctor should have quit while he was behind, but instead he came back with a second quip, 'Don't worry about a thing, you're in safe hands. We'll make sure we get the right eye. When I say the right eye I obviously mean the left eye. Or is it the right?'

I honestly thought Amy was going to punch him. Instead she expressed her hope that his surgical skills are better than his bedside manner and sent him on his way with a flea in his ear.

Once we were alone again, Amy sighed and looked up at me. 'You look tired.'

I sat on the edge of her bed. 'I am tired,' I confessed.

Amy shook her head and then quickly winced with pain. 'I feel like shit.'

'You look great. Your hair looks spectacular.' I really meant it.

'I thought you hadn't noticed,' she said.

'The last time I called you gorgeous it all went pear-shaped so I opted not to mention it this time,' I told her. I should have stopped there, but I didn't. 'Did one of the nurses cut it?'

'Does it look like a bloody nurse cut it?' Amy asked angrily. 'Just leave me alone, Graham.'

In my defence, your honour, I had never heard of hospitals having hairdressers attached to them before today.

Once I had managed to placate the woman I seemed to be doing a pretty good job of turning into my next ex, Amy and I chatted for a while about her operation and her fear of how she would look once the procedure had been completed. Eventually she will get a cosmetic replacement eye but she won't have that fitted until the swelling in her eye socket recedes. For a while, her eye socket won't look particularly attractive. I offered to buy her a pair of wrap-around sunglasses to cover the eye up. 'That's one way of ensuring you won't have to look at it I suppose,' Amy commented. I couldn't do right for doing wrong tonight.

Amy asked me how the party preparations were going. My birthday still hasn't been at the top of my list of priorities so I haven't done much in the way of preparation. I am not in the mood to celebrate. I haven't seen much of Lucy lately but I am not sure she will be up for it either. I suppose I should be pleased that Amy is still happy for the party to go ahead. 'Will you be out of here by a week on Friday?' I asked her.

'The doctors think I should be out, but who knows.' It goes without saying that I hope Amy is out well before my birthday.

Tonight's conversation hadn't gone according to plan. As I was leaving, I couldn't stop myself pushing once more.

'You do know how I feel about you, don't you?' I asked.

Her answer was fairly succinct. 'Graham, I need some space to concentrate on me. I need to love me again before I can let anyone else love me.'

I get it. I am just not very good at backing off.

Friday 19th September

The operation went as planned. Amy went in to the operating theatre with two eyes and came out with one. And the right one at that. I found this out from Imogen. In our phone conversation this evening, she once again suggested that I didn't come to the hospital for a few days. This time I listened. Imogen's advice wasn't given in a harsh way though. Her exact words were, 'Just give her a bit of space Graham. Once she has come to terms with her appearance, she will start noticing the things that are important to her again.'

Let's hope I am one of those things.

Amy doesn't want me seeing how she looks with one eye. From my point of view, I am sure the doctors will have done their best. I am getting my head around the idea. But it is easy for me. Not only does Amy have to get used to how she looks but she also has to get used to how other people will see her. I am determined to make her realise that she looks beautiful no matter what, but I am beginning to realise that it will take time.

Sunday 21st September

The boys are staying with me this weekend. It is Lucy's birthday on Tuesday and mine on Friday, the night of the joint party.

Jack has been panicking about what to get Lucy for her birthday. I have two boys and reckon there are few people in the world less qualified than me to answer questions about presents for fifteen-year-old girls. I therefore tried to get him to get some tips from his mother. His mother wasn't prepared to play though, telling him, 'Your dad is sleeping with her mother. Go and ask him.' I am not surprised she is a bit bitter after her recent interview with Messrs Bodie and Doyle or whatever they were called.

We ended up heading to Kingston in search of some inspiration this afternoon. Jack was up for the trip but Sean told me he would prefer to pull his toenails out with a pair of pliers. I had to bribe him with a promise of burgers and chocolate.

The best idea for a present I could come up with, but admittedly not the most original, was make-up or perfume. We went in to one shop and the assistant offered to spray a few samples on the boys' wrists to help Jack make his choice. 'You are joking, aren't you?' Sean said as he quickly backed out of the shop. I left with him, leaving Jack to fend for himself. Sean and I went in search of supplies for the party.

I had written a shopping list before we came out. It read:

1. Lager (approx. 20 over 18s – 150+ bottles)
2. White wine (6 bottles and then 4 boxes. People can drink the bottles first and then when they are too pissed to care, they can drink the boxed stuff)
3. Spirits – vodka for the ladies (2 bottles; no, 3, because Katie will drink one)
4. Orange juice – 12 cartons, for the vodka
5. Crisps – loads of assorted bags
6. Plastic glasses – big enough for vodka and orange but not so big that Katie can drink a pint of it in one go
7. Stain-remover for the inevitable spillages (note, Amy says no red wine because her shag pile is expensive)

We were wandering around the supermarket ticking things off as we went. As we passed the fizzy drinks, Sean asked what the kids were going to drink. Good question. We chucked a few bottles of Coke in. And a big birthday cake. Sean scoffed at the cake ('Lucy isn't four, dad.') but everyone loves a birthday cake, right?

'What am I going to do at this party, dad?' Sean asked as he was bundling more confectionary into the trolley.

'I don't know, eat loads of crap and drink Coke?' I asked. I had thought about Sean's participation myself too, particularly in light of the ground rules I had agreed with my ex. Sean won't want to mix with Lucy and her friends. He would be more capable of it than me but he won't want to do it. I wouldn't want to expose him to the adults either.

Even Jack has expressed a few reservations to me about the party. He might be as thick as thieves with Lucy but he is still socially awkward when it comes to girls in general. He is petrified of having to interact with Lucy's mates. And the dancing thing bothers him too. He really is a chip off the old block.

In the end I decided I would have to ask my ex to come and pick Sean up mid-way through the party, and possibly even Jack too if he feels he is standing out like a sore thumb. Both boys seemed happy enough with this proposal. I am not sure I should be giving my ex an excuse to be anywhere near the party but I actually feel quite relaxed about the situation. Amy's battle with injury has helped me put petty squabbles with my ex into context. They are unimportant in the grand scheme of things.

As we left the supermarket, I couldn't help thinking we had forgotten something. I phoned Imogen once I had dropped the children off at my ex's. She didn't sound too impressed as I listed the supplies I had got in for the party. 'Graham, leave the party planning to me,' Imogen said.

That was music to my ears.

Music. I had forgotten all about the music.

Tuesday 23ʳᵈ September

Today was a day of contrasts. On the one hand, Lucy celebrated her fifteenth birthday. She met Jack for a pizza after school and then her dad took her to the hospital to be with her mum.

On the other hand, Mrs F, Dave's mum, passed away in the night. I had thought about going round there today to call in on her but I was too late. Dave texted me this morning to give me the sad news. Dave and his dad were there when she died. She drifted off peacefully in her sleep. I feel for Dave. He will miss his mum. She suffered a bit towards the end so I bet he is relieved for her that her suffering is over.

Since I got his text this morning I have been half expecting Dave to phone me. When I last saw her back in April, Mrs F implied that Dave would discover some news after her death that would surprise him. She thought he might need my support. I still haven't got a clue what she was referring to but I am here for Dave. I texted him to tell him as much today.

I hadn't seen my mum and dad for a while until today. Because I had told them I was busy on my actual birthday (I hadn't told them quite what I was doing), they invited me over for a pre-birthday tea.

I walked to their house from work. As I stepped in

through the front door and into the kitchen, something felt different. Physically the house hasn't changed from when I had stayed there. The lamp in the hall was still plugged in to the faulty time switch which keeps it on all day and turns it off just as it gets dark. The fridge did its best to drown out conversation with its annoying hum and the bathroom door wouldn't shut properly after Jack had kicked it a couple of months ago.

Yet despite not changing, the house had somehow regained its charm. It felt like a home again rather than somewhere I had lodged while life went on around me. I have been back there a few times since I moved out, but it was only today that I really felt comfortable there again.

My mum had cooked cauliflower cheese and gammon, one of my favourites. Before the meal we raised a glass to Mrs F. My parents knew her too when I was growing up and would probably put in an appearance at the funeral.

After an appropriate pause for reflection, my parents turned their attention to me. 'How's life in your flat?' my dad asked. As conversation starters go, that felt like a fairly innocuous start.

'Oh, you know, I can come and go as I please.'

'Yes, but are you doing much coming and going, son?' he followed up.

'Dad, I'm doing OK,' I assured him. 'It is nearly six months since my divorce. In that time the boys have regained their mojo and I am not a grumpy dad as often as I used to be, so they seem happier spending time with me. My new job is more interesting than my last, and I have got my own flat. That can't be bad going in anyone's book, can it?' Counting my achievements off on my fingers like that felt pretty good to me. I glossed over the fitness-related objective though.

'That's great son, but are you happy?' my dad countered. He was like Albus when he gets a bone. He wouldn't drop it.

And then my mum joined in. The tag team at it again. 'And what about that woman you mentioned when you came to your father's seventieth? When do we get to meet her?'

I told my parents about Amy's accident and her subsequent recovery. I even told them about Jack and Lucy. They knew about Lucy already but not about her connection with Amy. I thought they would have a field day about that bit of gossip but they didn't. And I told them about mine and Amy's current issues - Amy's low self-esteem because of her damaged appearance and lost sight, my ex's interference in our affairs because of her jealousy, or to put a positive spin on it, her concern for her boys' upbringing, and my apparent inability to stop myself from saying the wrong thing.

'Amy sounds like a lovely woman. You should make sure you sort your differences out with her,' my mum advised. In that sentence, my mum moved on from fifteen years of showering my ex with praise to affirming her allegiance to Amy. That was the social worker in her kicking in, backing the injured victim. In this instance I didn't mind in the least.

But my mother hadn't finished yet. 'Tell us more about Amy,' she suggested. 'What does she do for a living?'

'She writes articles about sex,' I told my parents. I couldn't resist it.

'Does that mean she is good at it?' my dad asked.

Talking to my parents about Amy was therapeutic. If I can't talk to Amy, and I still can't at the moment because she is avoiding me, then the next best thing seems to be to talk to someone about Amy. The conversation made me realise yet again how important Amy has become to me. I have done pretty well in my quest to get a life but I won't consider my mission accomplished until Amy and I are together again.

Wednesday
24th September

Amy's mobile phone was smashed to pieces in the accident. As a consequence, I haven't been able to talk directly to her when I haven't been at the hospital. Most of my communication with Amy over the past six days has been third hand, via her mother. Tonight, Imogen phoned me from the hospital and passed the phone over to Amy. We exchanged pleasantries and then Amy gave me the bad news.

'They aren't sure I will be out of here by Friday night.'

'Why not? Everything is OK, isn't it?' I asked.

'Yes, everything is fine, but the doctors are still concerned by the headaches.'

Up until this point it was odds on that Amy would be let out in time for the party. Imogen has even bought a huge 'welcome home' banner and Jack and Lucy helped her put it up over the weekend in case Amy came home without much notice. The news that she won't be home is gutting, for me but also for Amy. She will miss her daughter's party (I expect that's how she thinks of it). To be frank, it won't be much of a party without Amy.

'I want to come and see you,' I said, almost pleadingly.

'Not yet, Graham,' Amy resisted, 'perhaps come at the weekend and tell me how the party went.' Well, that's something I suppose.

'Sergeant Atkinson has just been in to see me," she continued. "They have caught the driver who knocked me down.' Now this was really news. A small part of me tensed up as she talked. Was I about to hear something that would turn my world upside down again? Was she about to tell me that my ex had tried to kill her as part of some mad scheme to win me back or protect her children? Surely not.

It wasn't her. It was officially an accident rather than anything premeditated. Obviously I never thought for a minute that it was my ex.

Instead, it was just some woman with a bunch of misbehaving kids in the back of her car. She wasn't drunk, just distracted by a fight between her offspring. The woman handed herself in at Tooting police station this morning. She took her eyes off the road for a moment to shout at her children and that was all it took.

She should have stopped to do whatever she could do for Amy but I can understand her innate desire to protect her family unit. I haven't got the energy to stay angry at her. But that doesn't mean that I have forgiven her either. When I asked Amy how she felt, all she would say was, 'It probably could've happened to anyone but she left me bleeding on that road. Don't expect me to send the bitch a Christmas card.'

As soon as I had got off the phone from Amy, I phoned my ex. 'Helen, I can officially tell you that you are no longer a suspect in the investigation of the attempted murder of my Amy,' I told her.

'I should hope not too,' Helen said.

Helen is my ex. At the start of this diary I didn't want to name her because the diary was about me. It wasn't to be about her. That was the excuse I gave anyway. Looking back on it now, I think I was trying to turn my ex in to a non-person. Someone who didn't have a personality, who didn't even have a name. It suited me at the time to think of her as all bad, as someone at fault, someone to ridicule even.

The truth, of course, is less black and white. Helen has got a personality. She is in fact similar to me in a number of ways. She has her strengths and she has her weaknesses. As I have demonstrated over the course of this diary, so have I. We all have our faults. One of mine and Helen's faults was that we weren't very tolerant of each other. We took our time to discover that fact, and when we did discover it, we found we couldn't change. We got divorced. That is the simple truth.

I now feel confident enough in myself to admit that Helen isn't just a thing. She was an important part of my life for fifteen years and, as the mother of our children, she will continue to be important.

Being able to acknowledge Helen as a person again and not just as 'my ex' is probably an important step in the process of moving on in my life. Without overdoing it, I do feel liberated now that I have brought myself to share her name in this memoir. Will this mark a stage in our lives when I am not studying Facebook the next time my boys tell me there was a strange man in the house? Well, only time will tell I suppose.

Helen agreed to pick Sean up from the party on Friday night, and possibly even Jack too depending upon how he is finding it. With Amy not being there now, part of me feels that she might as well pick me up and drop me back at my flat too. This party could turn out to be a real damp squib.

Saturday 27th September

My forty-third birthday party has come and gone. Some people will remember it forever, some will want to forget it and others woke up this morning not being able to remember what they got up to last night. Needless to say, Katie is in the latter category.

When my alarm clock woke me up yesterday morning, I wanted to turn it off and go back to sleep. I can't remember ever having woken up on my own on my birthday before. In the last few years I have had my boys jumping on my bed thrusting presents at me within two minutes of the alarm going off. Not today, though.

I forced myself to shower and get dressed because I had agreed to help Imogen clean and prepare Amy's house for the party. The domestic help must have been given the day off again.

As I drove through Raynes Park and up to the Ridgeway, I couldn't bring myself to get excited about the events to come. This wasn't shaping up to be the party to end all parties. When I set out to sort my life out in six months, I had imagined that my birthday party would be a triumphant occasion at which my hordes of new friends would come together to celebrate my spectacular achievements and to toast my new-found conviviality.

Instead, it was looking like I would be playing second fiddle to a teenage girl, gate-crashing her birthday party, held at her mother's house while her mother avoids me in hospital. Woo-hoo.

Imogen was there waiting when I pulled the car on to Amy's drive. She gave me a birthday kiss on the cheek. When I didn't respond with a broad grin and a witty remark, she immediately got the measure of me.

'Now you listen to me, Graham, this is Lucy's big day. Despite her mother not being here to share it with her, Lucy has been talking about it for the last week. If she can cope with her mother being in hospital for her birthday, then so can you. Come on, I've got some jobs for you to do.' And off she marched in to the house.

As I mopped floors and scrubbed surfaces, I thought about Imogen's words. Yet again I had been too self-absorbed. This party isn't just about me. In fact it is mainly not about me. I owe it to Amy to make Lucy's day a success. I owe it to Lucy too. And to Jack and Sean. I gave myself another mental kick up the backside and got on with the mopping, the brushing, the toilet-cleaning, the heavy lifting and the plating of assorted confectionary.

Imogen had designated the kitchen and adjoining conservatory as the 'adults' zone' and the oak panelled dining room as the 'young people's zone', the idea being that the kids couldn't get to the alcohol in the kitchen fridge if they were restricted to the dining area.

I toiled long and hard to take most of the furniture out of the dining room, to provide the kids with a decent sized dance area. I am sure that pleased Jack.

By the time Lucy, and then Jack and Sean, arrived at Amy's from school, the dining table in their party room was laden with soft drinks and more sweet stuff than they could possibly eat. The sound system I had stolen from Helen's was also in place. I heard Jack telling Lucy that I might not be cool but at least I have cool speakers. I bet they won't be playing my music on them.

About an hour before the first guests arrived, Lucy went off to do what teenage girls do before parties and Jack and Sean sat watching some rubbish on Amy's cinema-sized telly. Imogen and I took the opportunity of this quiet moment to have a calming cup of tea and to take stock.

'Thanks for doing all this, Imogen,' I offered in the best conciliatory tone I could muster. I am in no doubt that the party wouldn't have happened without her energy and enthusiasm.

'Graham, it's my pleasure. More than anything I want to see young Lucy happy. It's her day.'

'She's a great kid.'

'I also want to see Amy happy,' Imogen continued. I sensed there was more to come so I just nodded while fiddling with the handle of my china cup.

'Are you the one to make her happy?' she asked. I felt like I was about to be interviewed for a job. It was a job I knew I wanted so I couldn't flunk the test. But having said that, a part of me didn't want to be having this conversation with Imogen. I wanted to be having it with Amy.

'Imogen, I want very much to make your daughter happy, but it's hard to do that when she doesn't want to see me.'

'Graham, don't you get it? It isn't that she doesn't want to see you. She doesn't want you to see her. Not looking like she thinks she does, anyway.'

'But that's just stupid,' I protested. 'Amy is the most glamorous, the most alluring, the most seductive person I have ever met. I can't take my eyes off her smile. A few scratches here and there isn't going to change that.'

Imogen put her hands up, indicating me to stop. 'It isn't me you should be telling this, is it?'

And then I got it. Grow a pair, Graham. Get off your arse. Get your backside in gear. Get your car in gear.

I grabbed my car keys off the kitchen side and ran out of the door without so much as a word to my boys about where I was going.

I sprayed gravel everywhere as I accelerated out of Amy's drive and up Parkside towards the A3. I drove as quickly as I could through the rush-hour traffic to the hospital. The adrenaline was flowing as I dumped the car on zigzag lines past the hospital entrance and ran in through the doors to the Atkinson Morley wing.

Had Amy simply been waiting for me to show her how little her injuries affected me? If so, then I have been a wimp, a pathetic excuse for a lover, making Amy and myself suffer unnecessarily. That was about to change. I was going to set the pace in a relationship for once in my miserable life.

I hurtled up three flights of stairs and ran through corridors, dodging all obstacles in my way until I reached Amy's ward. I didn't even hesitate. I barged straight in.

Amy's bed was empty. I stood there for a minute catching my breath and wiping the sweat from my forehead. Looking around, I saw that her bed was made. Her bedside locker still contained a few of Amy's knick knacks but her handbag was notable by its absence. I was about to open the travel case at the foot of the bed when Amy coughed. 'Are you after me?'

I turned around. Amy looked stunning. Dressed simply in jeans and a white long-sleeved top and a black leather jacket, she could have been a model. Her hair looked fantastic and the wrap-around sunglasses didn't look out of place. I expect my jaw dropped.

'I love you,' I muttered as I walked towards her. It was hardly a Paul Hogan to Linda Kozlowski in Crocodile

Dundee (I had a big crush on her) or Tom Hanks to Meg Ryan in Sleepless in Seattle (I had a crush on her too). My Shakespeare deserted me too, so I just stuck with the simple-is-best approach.

I took Amy's sunglasses off and kissed her. And kissed her again. And then she kissed me back and we held each other, tighter and tighter until she winced. In the heat of the moment I had forgotten entirely about her injuries.

I will always relive that moment in my mind, the moment I stopped being a total wuss and manned up. The moment when I totally let go of my inhibitions and laid my emotions bare in front of Amy. I will never forget her reaction, her joy at knowing that I wanted her, and her now, not her as she was before the accident. I will never forget the moment I got a life.

We stayed standing, entwined in each other's arms, for quite some time. Eventually, Amy asked if we were going to the party.

'Are we going?' I asked incredulously. 'You haven't been discharged, have you?'

'Why do you think I have got my jacket on?' she asked. 'The doctors have given me permission to come home for the night. I was on my way to the lift when I saw you coming from the other direction.' The night was getting better and better.

Amy and I made our way back to my car which, miraculously, hadn't been towed away. The journey home was much more leisurely than my dash to the hospital an hour earlier had been. Amy and I didn't say much to each other. For my part, I was getting my head around having Amy with me this evening. And Amy was just looking forward to coming home.

As we pulled in through the gates, we could hear the

monotonous thud of modern bass-heavy music blasting out of the open dining room window. Unsurprisingly, Lucy's music was drowning out whatever was being played by the adults in the back of the house.

'Where do you want to go first?' I asked as we walked towards the front door. Amy stopped me and kissed me again. As we were kissing, the front door opened, throwing light on to us standing in the porch. People burst out of the house seemingly from every direction and surrounded us. Amy detached herself from me and hugged her daughter and her mother. Jack hugged me. As I wiped a tear from my eye, Sean told me to stop being such a sissy. A drink was thrust in to my hand, I think by Dave who had turned up despite his mother dying a few days ago.

I felt incredibly happy.

Eventually Lucy led her mother back in to the house and everyone gradually followed. Most of the teenagers drifted off back into the dining room and the monotonous beat started up again, only quieter in consideration of Amy's fragile head. Lucy, Amy and the rest of the adults sat in the conservatory.

I looked around. Dave was there, as were Bryan and Katie, although they weren't sitting together. John and Tracey were there, although they weren't sitting anywhere near Bryan and Katie. Ray was there, and he was sitting next to Mr Def Leppard from my upstairs flat. That was interesting.

Hills and Donna were there too. Hills was drinking from a vodka bottle so I reckon it must be Donna that's pregnant.

All in all, there was a good turnout to celebrate my spectacular achievements and to toast my new-found conviviality. I was even thinking of getting up and making a speech. Luckily for me, and for everyone around me, someone put the music back on.

Stevie Wonder's 'Happy Birthday'.

'Who put that shit on?' I asked, outraged that anyone would think I am old enough to remember Stevie Wonder.

'Do you know who sings this song?' Amy piped up as people looked at me awkwardly.

'Stevie Wonder,' I responded, thinking, 'what am I missing?'

'And what's he?' she asked me with a glint in her eye.

'I don't know, about 70?'

'He is blind,' Imogen said, from beside the stereo.

'So is that guy who used to be the Home Secretary,' I said, 'but it doesn't mean I have to listen to him.' And then I suddenly got where they were going with this. Amy was looking for inspiration from people who couldn't see very well but had continued to make a success of their lives.

'That nice man who played Columbo only had one eye' Imogen pointed out.

In an attempt to bolster Amy's confidence still further, I tried another one. 'Wasn't that England goalie blind in one eye?'

'Gordon Banks lost an eye in a car crash and had to retire,' Bryan corrected me. I shut up then.

'Homer was blind too,' Hills joined in.

'Homer isn't blind!' Jack protested. I hadn't noticed him come in.

'Homer the ancient Greek poet, not Homer Simpson you chump,' Hills explained, ruffling Jack's hair, much to his disgust.

'And you know one-eyed people can drive.' This one from Sean.

'You are all too good to me,' Amy managed to mutter through her tears.

The party continued late into the night. Other notable events included Katie punching Bryan and then falling out of the conservatory doors in to a raised flower bed, Dave talking to my ex Helen and going off in the car with her and Sean, Jack throwing up in the aforementioned raised flower bed ('it must have been the dodgy pizza') and Amy telling me she loved me too.

Diary note

I set myself the challenge of getting my life sorted out by my birthday. This was of course a bit of a hypothetical challenge. Can any of us say that our lives are fully sorted out? People prone to clichés say that life is a journey. Enjoy the good bits of the ride, because there are bound to be a few bad bits coming up at some point in the future. Another cliché that is particularly apt in my case is that life is a rollercoaster. I am enjoying the up but as sure as night follows day, there will be a down soon. I think I'll quit writing while I am ahead.

If you have enjoyed reading 'Six Months to Get a Life' then let me whet your appetite for my next book, 'Six Lies'.

Prologue

Dear David,

It has been said before but I will say it again. Rectal cancer is a pain in the backside.

If you are reading this letter then the wretched disease has got the better of me. As I sit here in my bedroom scribbling away, I know my time is running out. I have fought my heart out over the past couple of years to fend off my cancer but life is too painful. I am beginning to run out of fight. Once I have finished this letter, I plan to accept any drugs on offer and drift off quietly into oblivion. My time has come.

I have spent time over the past few days reflecting upon what difference I have made to the world. This may sound a bit old hat but believe me, when you know you will be dying soon, the urge to look back rather than think about a future you won't be part of is irresistible.

I have never wanted fame and fortune. I won't be studied by generations of school children or idolised by thousands of sports fans. I don't suppose even the music world will mourn my passing despite me being the best sax player in London back in the day.

None of that matters to me though. Without a doubt, your dad's and my greatest contribution to this world is you.

You are a joy to be around and a positive influence on every-one you meet. When you walk into a room, people notice. Your enthusiasm for life is infectious. Everyone you meet falls in love with you. You didn't achieve your dream of being the next Billy Joel or Liverpool's record striker but even if you had, your father and I wouldn't have been more proud of you than we already are. We love you more than you could ever know and I for one will go to my grave in the knowledge that I have brought up a unique, sparky and fun-loving son.

I am truly sorry to be leaving you. My heart aches because I will never again get to share a pot of tea with you on your way home from work. I won't get to play cards with you and your dad or discover new restaurants with the pair of you. I won't get to hear about all those scrapes you get yourself into on a regular basis. I won't get to meet your next 'chosen one'. On that subject, don't you think it is about time you actually chose another woman to settle down with rather than just choosing one for the night?

This letter would have been worth writing even if it was only to tell you how proud I am of you. But unfortunately there is something else I need to say to you.

There is no easy way to say this so I will just come out with it. Biologically-speaking, I am not your mother.

Those words must be truly shocking to you. I can imagine your sharp intake of breath. I bet you uttered a swear word or two. Of course I don't blame you.

Your father can tell you the full story. To be fair to your dad, he has always wanted you to know. It is me that stopped him from telling you our secret. All I can say to you is that I kept the truth from you for the right reasons. I have always loved you as if you were my own son. I couldn't have cared more for you if I had tried. I didn't want you to find out that you weren't my flesh and blood because I didn't want you ever doubting my love for you.

You are a strong man, David. You have coped with adversity in the past. I know you can cope with this news too. You are sur-

rounded by good friends. If you need to, talk to Graham about this news. He will help you through it.

I don't know what else to say now. Do you remember you used to come home from school every Wednesday and tell me how many goals you scored in your school football game? And then one Wednesday you came home really excited and said, 'mum, mum, I really scored a goal today!'

I love you son.

Mum

CPSIA information can be obtained at www.ICGtesting.com
Printed in the USA
BVOW07s1015030215

386157BV00004B/115/P